Rich Chick

The "Nine Must–Have Accessories" Every Girl Needs to Create Financial Confidence, Independence and Freedom the Smart Way

By Michelle Matson

Published by:
Michelle Matson
5955 Deerfield Blvd,
Mason, OH 45040

ISBN: 0-932767-05-3

Printed in the United States of America

This publication is designed to provide accurate and authoritative information with
regard to the subject matter covered. It is sold with the understanding that the
publisher is not engaged in rendering legal, accounting, or other professional
advice. If legal advice or other expert assistance is required, the services of a
competent professional person should be sought.
– From a *Declaration of Principles* jointly adopted by a Committee of the American
Bar Association and a Committee of Publishers and Associations.

This book is available at quantity discounts for bulk purchases.
For information, call 513–204–8000.

For two generations of Chicks who make my life Richer:

Linda, Mary Lou,

Lexi, Riley, and Reece

Table of Contents
Introduction

Acknowledgements

I always feel like the acknowledgments section is like the Oscar-winning speech. I hope I do justice to all of the people who have helped me with this project. Thank you to everyone who has been supportive and helped me figure out what a Rich Chick is. So, here it goes...

A big, huge thank you to my editor extraordinaire, Ginny McCabe, thank you for taking my endless parentheses and ellipsis and turning them into coherent thoughts that have style, sass, and sense.

To my husband, Matt, who makes it possible to do what I love and still be a wife and a mom. I'm very lucky to have you and our family, and I'm very grateful for the good things we have in our life.

To my girls, Lexi, Riley, and Reece who make me feel good about going to work and always compliment my shoes and clothes when I dress up in the morning. Thank you for not complaining too much when I'm a tired, grumpy mommy. I hope that someday this book will help you be strong, brave, independent women and have the life you want.

To Mark Matson, who has generously educated me about investing for the last 17 years. Thank you for being the best coach and mentor I could ask for and bringing me along on the adventure of saving investors. We have accomplished so much, and I know that we have so much more to contribute. I can't wait to see what we can do next.

To my parents Mike and Linda, thanks for raising me to be independent, think for myself, work hard, and do what needs to be done. I hope that can teach my girls those same things.

To my guinea chicks: Linda, Kim, Melissa, Kelly, and Lauren. Thank you for reading the early versions of Rich Chick, believing in it, and giving me the support, pep talks, and encouragement I needed to keep making it better. I'm very lucky to have girlfriends like you.

Thank you to our entire team at Matson Money, what an amazing group of people who not only do a great job every day, but have fun doing it. Thank you to all the ladies of Matson Money who read early versions and gave great, constructive feedback. Alaine, Lindsey, Nicole, Shannon, and Rene, thank you for bringing this puppy down the home stretch and making it look fabulous in the process. Jennifer, thank you for the patience and creativity you bring to RichChick.com, and for smiling every time we re-tweak. Ken – thank you for keeping me on my toes and not letting my typos get the best of me. Zack, thanks for being the go-to-guy for numbers and a good laugh.

I want to acknowledge and thank the wonderful financial advisors who I have the privilege to know and work with through Matson Money. Your commitment to your clients is inspiring and gives me hope for many people to take control of their financial futures and have the investment success they deserve. Special thanks to Phyllis Wordhouse, Maureen Verduyn, and Leonard Raskin who meticulously read the manuscript, and gave generous feedback and comments.

My apologies to anyone I've left off the list, you are not forgotten and I sincerely appreciate you!

Michelle

Introduction

Investing is a great thing that anyone can do—especially women. By accessorizing your life with helpful hints, tips and strategies, you'll soon discover that it might not be as difficult as you think to become a successful investor and the "Rich Chick" that you've always dreamed of becoming.

Throughout this book you'll find a number of ideas and innovative suggestions on how to wisely invest your money. You'll find that building and growing wealth through investing can be attained in a variety of ways. And as a result of reading this book, you will be able to make educated and informed choices about money, such as how much you should save, and when and where to invest your money.

Let's get started. I am always drawn to stories, movies and television shows that revolve around strong, independent women. I'm a classic chick-flick junkie. I love to see girls and women succeed, especially when they face overwhelming obstacles to overcome in order to become successful. For this reason I would like to help you implement several key principles that will help pave the way for you now and in the future to gain financial freedom and build wealth.

As we take a look at some basic money principles, you'll have an opportunity to take charge of your life and make the most out of your financial resources by implementing the ***Nine Rich Chick Must-Have Accessories*** in your life. I have three daughters whom I hope will grow into self-sufficient, confident, independent women. The best way to help them accomplish this is to show them how it can be done and to lead them by example. My daughters are continually watching every move I make. In the same way, the strategies shared in this book will work equally well for you, my daughters and for anyone.

Are you ready to gain the confidence and freedom that goes along with creating your own financial independence? Being a "Rich Chick" is not simply about "getting rich," but it is more about learning how you can put your money to work so that you can accomplish your dreams.

Investing doesn't have to be a somber and stodgy subject, although at times it can be a serious and overwhelming topic. But the investing process can be fascinating and fun, too. My goal is to help you learn and apply several basic strategies and concepts so that you can become a "Rich Chick" who has control of her financial future. Throughout each of the chapters, you will learn more about what it takes to do that and how to turn these money-saving strategies into real-life results.

Each of us can relate to topics we love—shopping, clothes, shoes, purses, fancy food, cooking and other girl stuff, which will be covered throughout the book using a variety of different examples as it relates to money and our lifestyles. You will learn about practical and effective ways to "accessorize" your financial future, and after executing these ideas, you'll be well-equipped with the things you need to become a successful investor. Get ready to accessorize your life as you discover the fundamentals of how simple it is to become a Rich Chick.

Once Upon A Time-There Is Power In Your Dreams

Always believe in your dreams. As women, we all hold on to some fairy tale or fantasy that we longed for as children. We still want to marry a prince, live in a castle and have beautiful gowns with matching shoes; although our fantasies change as we grow older, and hopefully your spouse is your prince and your home is your castle. Dreams are one aspect of our lives that keep us moving forward—in our personal endeavors, home lives, with our families and in our careers. We can also apply our dreams to how we handle money.

While some things never change, nothing ever really stays the same. Dreams are much bigger than "stuff." Don't get me wrong, we love the "stuff" and want to acquire things that help us lead more fulfilling and rich lives, but there is much more to becoming successful women than our material possessions. As women who are wives, mothers, sisters and daughters, there are many goals and dreams we want to accomplish, and typically all of those things are going to require one thing—money.

It doesn't matter how big our dream is. We may have simple dreams or huge ones; but the dream itself is the first key to creating financial independence. Our dreams give us the drive and motivation to achieve our goals.

Once we understand what our dreams are and we find the motivation to achieve them, things will begin to happen that will help us succeed. I hope you have big, giant, crazy dreams...because the bigger and wilder they are, the more motivated you will become in making your dreams come true. My hope is that I can help you eliminate the money obstacle and gain financial freedom so that you will ultimately fulfill all of your dreams. Once we define what our dreams are, we can take practical steps toward achieving them. And as we achieve them, we can continue to set new goals and ensure ourselves of a bright financial future.

Who Is A Rich Chick?

A Rich Chick is someone who is ready to create her own financial future. She knows that she is the only one who can establish her future. She is someone who is willing to do whatever it takes to make the most of her money and her investments. A Rich Chick is responsible for her own money and is willing to put time and effort into getting her financial house in order. At the same time, she has better things to do with her time and energy than to monitor daily market swings or to follow the investment media around the clock. As a Rich Chick, you'll be able to rest easy, have financial peace and focus on other important aspects of your life.

There are nine distinct qualities or "accessories" that set a Rich Chick apart from other women. We will discuss these here and help you discover each accessory within yourself. By using the Rich Chick Method, you will be able to eliminate the stress and fears related to your financial future.

The Nine Rich Chick Must-Have Accessories Are:

- **Inquisitiveness -** Your beliefs and values are at the core of who you are, and many of those beliefs and values you learned as a child. As adults, we incorporate our beliefs and values into ideas that yield either positive or negative results. Being inquisitive means you can have total control over your money decisions. You can choose how to deal with the money demons that haunt you, and evolve into a healthy lifestyle that will allow you to create fun and powerful ways to handle your money. Ultimately, the wise decisions you make will positively impact your future.

- **Purpose -** Your True Purpose for Money is bigger than money itself – it's your true purpose for everything that motivates you in life. Use your True Purpose to motivate your best money decisions.

- **Future-Focused** – Wandering aimlessly through life will only get you so far. If you have big dreams, it is critical to be specific about when, where and how you are going to accomplish them. Create a "Future You" map that will give you focus and direction for achieving your goals.

- **Determination** - Determination is the one accessory that will single-handedly take us farther than any other Rich Chick Must-Have Accessory. No matter what kind of Rich Chick you are, determination will provide the kind of stamina that will drive you throughout your Rich Chick journey. Life is full of twists and turns; that's why we need to be determined beyond the day-to-day and learn to look at how our choices will impact the bigger picture down the road.

- **Discipline** – If it were easy everyone would be rich. It takes a little self-control and discipline to do what needs to be done. You have to pay yourself first and protect your future like a ferocious mama bear.

- **Savvy** - A Rich Chick is Savvy about her investment choices. She is well-informed and perceptive when it comes to her financial future. She makes financial decisions based on solid information that will last long-term.

- **Intelligence** - Use the intelligence of the true experts of economics and investing when it comes to your financial future; don't rely on predictions or fortune-tellers.

- **Commitment** - Sticking to the rules isn't always easy, but a Rich Chick sees the bigger picture and has the will to stick with the program.

- **Coachability** - It's easier to be accountable to someone beyond yourself. A good investor coach will help keep you on the right track even when the going gets rough.

Just like putting together the perfect outfit, figuring out the perfect portfolio and investment plan for you begins with the ***Nine Rich Chick Must-Have Accessories.*** Once you start with the basics, like your little black dress, you can build upon those fundamentals to create your own look, feel and personality as you choose the appropriate accessories. A successful investing experience starts by taking the first steps. By adding the appropriate "accessories," you will begin to build your portfolio.

Because we all have dreams and the ability to deal with our finances in powerful ways, I believe anyone can become a Rich Chick. A Rich Chick is never defined by her age. Whether you're in your 20's or in your 60's, you can find the confidence, independence and financial security you need to become a Rich Chick.

Finding the Rich Chick inside of you will enrich your life in so many ways. Being "rich" will give you control and total command of your financial future. Soon, all of your future money worries will melt away into a faint memory. Ultimately, becoming a Rich Chick will give you peace of mind.

Though everyone is not going to become a millionaire, no matter what level of financial success you achieve, you'll soon feel like a million bucks by knowing exactly where you are and where you are headed financially. This financial peace will give you a greater sense of direction and it will help you make better decisions about your money on a daily basis.

The Rich Chick Method is not about having more money than your friends or coworkers, nor is it about comparing what you have to everyone else. You may have more, or you may have less. But in the end, by taking a few practical and attainable steps, you will have done everything possible to maximize your own wealth.

Everyone will not start out, or even end up, equally because there are many different factors that determine our wealth, such as income, savings, expenses, debt, the number of investments you have and so on. These factors will impact the math of your individual journey, and that is okay. Your ultimate goal should be to make the most of what you have.

You're Not Cinderella-And There's No Fairy Godmother Or Prince Coming to Save You

As a Rich Chick, your financial success depends upon you. In reality, you can't solely depend on someone else to make things happen for you. Having a fairy tale expectation from any relationship or person is only asking for disaster because it's not based on reality. Never wait on a white knight or a prince to come to the rescue in regard to your finances. Finding him won't make all of our woes, financial or otherwise, go away. My husband is definitely my "prince" and he makes my life more fulfilling and complete, but I do not expect him to be responsible for me like a "damsel in distress," especially when it comes to our finances. We are partners in managing our family's financial resources. In fact, I might be a little more in-tune with the state of our overall finances than he is.

When it comes down to it, you are the only person who can make sure you have exactly what you need financially. It's up to you, sister. Whether you are married, single, divorced, working, not working, or whatever your situation is, it's up to you. You are one hundred percent responsible for your financial situation. Sometimes it is easy for us to complain about our own circumstances. But we should always be ready for the unexpected things that are bound to come up in our lives. We don't have total control over everything that happens to us all of the time. For example, our car might break down and leave us with expensive repair bills, or our purse may get stolen and our credit cards may get charged up. We can't escape life's unexpected surprises, but we can learn to be prepared for them. No matter what happens, it comes down to the decisions we make, and doing the best with what we have.

One safeguard that can help is to factor in a little extra money in our budgets to help cover us during rough times by including something like a "rainy day" fund, or an amount of spare cash that is set aside for emergencies. Whatever the safeguard, our main focus should be how we will align our financial future and what we are going to do to keep it on track. We can't blame others for our bad breaks. Life is going to happen. The good news is there are steps we can all take to safeguard our financial success in spite of unexpected setbacks or unforeseen failures that are going to happen to each of us from time to time.

It wouldn't be much fun to spend your golden years sitting around, blaming everyone else for your misfortune. Monkey wrenches are a part of life and we must deal with them appropriately. When I retire I plan on sitting in my summer home, spending time with my husband, our children and grandchildren. I don't want to think about any money woes at all. I fully believe that if we are smart with our money now, we will do well in preparing for our future and retirement years. The key to success is creating a plan and sticking to it. Being a Rich Chick requires a particular mind-set and perspective. This methodology is for women who are willing to take accountability for themselves and for their finances, even if it becomes uncomfortable at times.

Becoming a Rich Chick takes time, energy and commitment. And the more time you have the better. Your financial freedom won't happen overnight. In this book, you will set immediate, intermediate and long-term goals that will help you measure and reward your successful transformation into a Rich Chick. It is never too early or too late to get on the Rich Chick path. The earlier the better and that is the key to growing your wealth quickly. And, the sooner you begin the more wealth you will acquire. If you are in your 20's or 30's you have plenty of time to gather your wealth and grow it into something you could have never imagined.

However, if you are in your 40's, 50's or older, don't be discouraged. You can still take steps that will prepare you for your retirement years. You'd be amazed at what a difference just a few years of investing can do for your retirement. While it may be more difficult to attain a million-dollar portfolio the later you start; it is still possible for you to prepare for the future.

Getting Started Is Easy

By picking up this book and desiring to learn more about becoming financially free, you have taken the first steps toward creating your own financial independence. You have already proven that you have the motivation and determination to begin making vital changes. Now your financial and investing education can begin. Education starts with awareness, and your decisions and actions matter greatly when it comes to managing your money. We've already talked a lot about awareness in these first few pages. By simply having and developing your interest in money, finances and investing, you are ahead of the curve and are now positioned for greater success.

This process is going to provide you with the confidence you need to properly handle the financial aspects of your life, as well as many other areas of your life. By completing these exercises and utilizing these Rich Chick strategies, you will gain greater control of your money and effectively direct your financial future. It can be scary when you realize that finances are your responsibility. But on the flip side, with that responsibility comes empowerment and growth. And as it is with most areas of our lives, we feel better when we know exactly where we're headed. When it comes to money and finances, you won't have to stumble around in the dark anymore. You will soon have a firm grasp on what you are doing with your money and why. If you haven't started already, you will begin to lay a foundation and establish the groundwork for a prosperous future.

Once you've made the commitment to accept this responsibility, give yourself a pat on the back. The quality of your life is about to improve. Now you will not only begin to help yourself, but you will be able to share the wealth of knowledge you've gained with your family, friends and others. It feels great to be in charge of your own destiny, doesn't it? Along the journey, I hope to help you find that pot of gold at the end of the rainbow. Be encouraged, because it is within your reach. Becoming a Rich Chick will take you down the path of fulfilling your dreams and will enable you to love life and experience it to the fullest. As an investment coach and mentor, and as a Rich Chick myself, I am so happy we are on this path of discovery together. Sit back and relax, because it's going to be fun. Get ready for some girl talk that peeks into your heart, mind and wallet as we uncover tips, helpful hints and advice that will direct your financial future.

Chapter One

Inquiring Minds Want to Know...

Rich Chick Must-Have Accessory #1: Inquisitive

We all have weird and quirky hang-ups about money. The funny thing is that most of these habits and beliefs were developed when we were young children. Maybe you grew up with parents who had to struggle financially, or were raised by a single working mom, or perhaps you were given everything you ever wanted. We all have a unique story to tell about how our families dealt with money when we were growing up. Those behaviors influence how we feel about and manage our money today. In this chapter, we are going to investigate Rich Chick Must-Have Accessory #1: Inquisitive by inquiring and reflecting on ourselves, and taking a deeper look at who we are. We'll also learn to ask ourselves some life-changing questions about what makes us who we are and where we're headed in regard to our philosophies about money and where our past, present and future ideas about money can take us. Now, let's take a look at Angie's story. Read about what she experienced, and what it took for her to become inquisitive. Then, we'll learn how you can do it, too.

Real-Life Rich Chick: Angie

Meet Angie. Angie is a friend of mine who grew up in a typical middle-class family. Her dad was the breadwinner and her mom stayed at home to take care of their kids. Angie's dad took care of everything financially, including earning the money and paying the bills. He did it all.

As a young adult, Angie had always struggled with getting her finances in order. She was frequently paying her bills late, building up a lot of credit card debt, and when she began her career, she didn't consider saving for retirement. Then, Angie's dad suddenly passed away. Within a few short weeks, Angie watched her mom struggle with the loss of her husband, with no idea about how to take care of herself financially. Her mom had no income of her own, no money stashed away, and no idea what investments or retirement arrangements her husband had previously made.

Seeing her mom become so helpless and frantic made Angie angry and frustrated. The death of her father helped Angie realize that she had been dealing with her finances in the same way her mom had all of these years, which was not dealing with them at all.

She was avoiding getting involved and assuming that the person she would marry someday would handle her finances.

In order to help out her mom, Angie stepped in and began digging through all of her parents' financial records to find out what her father had done with their investments and retirement monies, to help her mom get on the right track. As her mom became more familiar with her checkbook and bank accounts, Angie watched her mom gain a confidence and an independence, which she had never known before.

At that point in her life, Angie recognized that she too had been living with the attitude that it was someone else's job to take care of her financially. She also acknowledged that if she didn't do something about it, this would ultimately leave her feeling the same way her mom felt—helpless. Angie realized that taking control of her finances meant that she was taking charge of her future and her independence. Now Angie understands the value of squashing out her money demons and is investing in her future.

Most of the time, we don't associate our current money managing techniques with our childhood experiences. But, when we take a closer look at our money roots, they reveal a lot about us. We relate money to our values and habits. And what we learned as children influences our attitude about money today.

Our knowledge and understanding of money evolves from the world around us, the environment we live in, and from our culture. These influences form our beliefs about money. We are born into a culture where we are automatically exposed to an established set of beliefs about money and wealth. Every television show, movie, news program, magazine, newspaper and billboard we see conveys subtle, and sometimes not-so-subtle, messages about how to deal with, spend, save or invest our money. Now it's time to figure out how all of those messages affect us every day.

Messages about money are everywhere. Throughout our lives, we have been exposed to numerous money messages, which have become ingrained in us. My favorite money message, "Money doesn't grow on trees" is one that has been passed down through the ages. If I had a penny for every time my mom said that, I would be rich. Below I've started a list of money messages that I've heard, with room for you to fill in your favorites too.

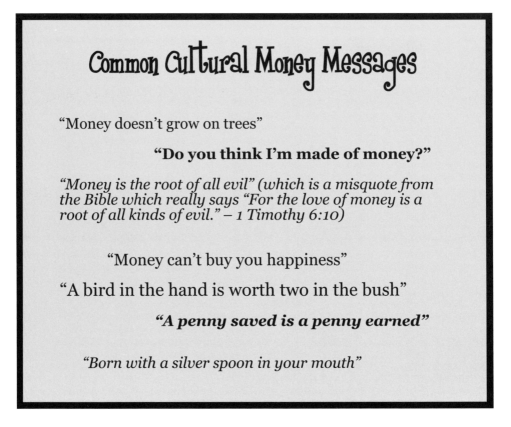

Common Cultural Money Messages

"Money doesn't grow on trees"

"Do you think I'm made of money?"

Money is the root of all evil" (which is a misquote from the Bible which really says "For the love of money is a root of all kinds of evil." – 1 Timothy 6:10)

"Money can't buy you happiness"

"A bird in the hand is worth two in the bush"

"A penny saved is a penny earned"

"Born with a silver spoon in your mouth"

"Don't have two nickels to rub together"

"Filthy rich"

"A fool and his money are soon parted"
"Penny wise and pound foolish"

"Put your money where your mouth is"

"There's no such thing as a free lunch"

"Time is money"

"Money isn't everything"

"Spend it while you've got it"

"You can't take it with you"

"The rich get richer..."

Now make a list of the ones you've heard:

_____

_____

_____

_____

_____

_____

_____

When we stop and think about how our personal habits and beliefs about money are formed, we'll see how the beliefs that we developed early in life are still hanging around and messing with us in regard to the decisions we are currently making about money. Although we'll admit we are trying to be different and avoid some of the negative things we were taught, we all know that the things we learned as children have an impact on us in some way today.

Family Stories About Wealth And Poverty

I grew up in an average middle class, blue-collar family. We lived in a small town in a wonderful house that my parents literally built with their own hands. While I don't remember any specific stories about my grandparents or great-grandparents relating to their money and wealth, I don't think that there was any notable amount of wealth in our family history to speak of. However, I do remember one time when my family felt an economic pinch. When I was about six years old, something in our house changed. I didn't know what was happening at the time, but there was a distinct shift in the climate of our household. My dad's construction business, which had operated out of a building across the street from my school, suddenly moved into our basement. My mom began helping out with the business, which I never noticed her doing before, and my grandma started making a lot of my clothes, and she was no fashion designer. Yes, there was a lot of polyester involved, which made them nearly indestructible – the thought of them still makes me shudder. Although I didn't know all of the specifics, I was aware on some level that something was different in our household, and that it made my parents feel stressed and unhappy.

We all have our own stories that have shaped us, and made us into who we are as adults. Our experiences can make us stronger, or they can break us down. Whatever our stories are, there are life lessons in all of them, and traditions that help carry them from generation to generation.

Tell your own story here:

_____

_____

_____

_____

_____

What kinds of things do you remember hearing from your parents about money? What were their beliefs and how did they deal with them? I think that one of my dad's favorite sayings was, "It's only money." I don't consider him to be a big spender, but he doesn't obsess about money either.

I have the most amazing mother-in-law ever, who grew up in the "hollers" of West Virginia with very little money. She laughs when she tells me what her mother told her, "It's not a sin to be poor, but it's a sin to be dirty." That always makes me smile, because one of my mother-in-law's favorite things to do is clean. She clearly adopted that belief from her childhood. She put a positive spin on it, and it works for her.

Write down your perception of your parents' beliefs about money:

Mom's Beliefs:

_____

_____

_____

_____

_____

Dad's Beliefs:

_____

_____

_____

_____

_____

Which of these ideas or beliefs have you adopted into your adult life? How have they affected your thoughts about money, spending habits and saving decisions? Which of these things do you believe have influenced you, and how have you either continued the pattern or changed your parents' beliefs about money?

_____

_____

_____

_____

_____

_____

_____

As a child, did you ever worry or complain about money? I remember wanting name brand clothes, and all of the same popular toys that my friends had. I would have countless conversations with my mom about how she thought that those things were too expensive. Sometimes, I was given the things I wanted, but on other occasions I had to wait. I think those early lessons helped me figure out what I really wanted. I also learned that there are times when I might have to save up for something in order to get it. What's your story about what you thought about money as a child? And what did you tell yourself when you were upset or frustrated? Think about the times when you didn't get what you wanted. Most importantly, what did you learn? Has what you learned as a child been helpful to you, or has it hindered you?

_____

_____

_____

_____

_____

_____

_____

Now, think back to your first experiences with money: your first job, car, or to the time when you opened your first bank account. What did you learn about money from those early experiences? I started a very lucrative four-year babysitting career in the sixth grade. I was busy every weekend watching kids for my parents' friends, so I earned a fair amount of spending money for a young teen. At 14, I got a "real job" at a small grocery store where I worked as a cashier, selling produce for two years. Ah, the smell of apples in the fall still gives me goose bumps. I was hired under minimum wage, making two dollars an hour, and I thought that I was making a lot of money. I clocked about 20 hours a week at the grocery store and I continued to babysit on the side, so I had a decent income for a high school student.

When I started driving at age 16, my parents gave me my mom's 1981 Maroon Chevy Monte Carlo with T-tops, which were so heavy and hard to take out that I rarely did. I was responsible for paying for my own insurance and for gas. And, since I had a job, when I got to the age where it was important to have the same clothes everyone else had, I started buying my own clothes. Early on, I learned to be self-sufficient and to save for the things that were important to me, and that philosophy has continued to work well for me throughout my adult life.

What first, real-life experiences have you had with money? What was your first job, car, bank account, credit card, etc.? What did you learn from those experiences?

_____

_____

_____

_____

_____

Rich People

We all have preconceived notions when we think about or hear the words "rich people." I think everyone has a gut reaction when they think about people who are rich. Think about those notable, extremely rich people, like movie stars, actresses, famous musicians, athletes and corporate CEOs. When you think about their money and how rich you think they are, what is your initial gut reaction about how much money they have?

Rich people are...(Finish the sentence):

_____

_____

You might say something like they are "lucky" or "snobs" or something equally unrelated to the character, integrity or success of the individuals you're talking about. Many times people have a negative interpretation about people who they consider to be rich. This might be based on jealousy or on some other emotion that has no rational basis, since most of us don't personally know the people we're talking about. If we have a negative interpretation about people who we consider to be rich, it prevents us from doing what we need to do to become rich, because who wants to be called a "rich snob" or someone who "got lucky" and didn't earn what they have? This is the moment to give up any garbage or negative thoughts we have about rich people. Chances are that anyone who we consider to be rich did something to get that way–they worked hard, earned it, had good fortune, won the lottery, or they did whatever they needed to do to get there.

My Money Beliefs

Now go back and review everything you've written down in the writing on previous pages above that reflect upon your money beliefs. After you review them, try to come up with a summary about what you believe. Some aspects of it might be positive and others might be negative, but either way it's okay. The important thing is to be honest about your personal money beliefs.

Ex: *"Don't lend money to relatives."*

Once you have identified your beliefs about money, you will begin to see how they can affect your relationship with money. Some beliefs may be positive, and will be helpful in dealing with the various aspects of your finances, but other beliefs may cause significant problems, relative to money.

The more you understand about your own money beliefs, the more power you will have to make grounded financial decisions. We're going to look at how you can determine if these beliefs have a positive or a negative impact on your overall financial landscape.

No matter what you believe, your money beliefs have become truths to you. So, how do you know if your beliefs are positive or negative? The first telltale sign of a negative belief is if it shows up as a persistent complaint related to money in your life. You will not find humor in your negative beliefs about money, and when you are caught up in them, they will drain you of energy. As a result, they can cause you to become very self-involved, stressed and you might even feel helpless.

Positive money beliefs are different, because when you think of money matters in a favorable light, you will feel good about yourself. When it comes to money matters, certain beliefs will give you confidence and energy and allow you to see and experience the responsible aspects of dealing with money. Positive money beliefs will give you the power and peace of mind that you need to become successful. Once you identify your positive money beliefs, you can use them like your favorite lipstick and pull them out as needed. You can also put them on like you would a pearl, diamond or your favorite necklace, and they will continue to help you make right choices about your money.

Now that you know how to differentiate between positive and negative money beliefs, go back to your beliefs list and mark each one with either a (+) for positive or a (-) for negative. We're going to use this information more later, as we continue throughout this chapter.

Whining And Complaining

As human beings, we all like to whine and complain about the things that annoy us. We spend time gossiping with our girlfriends about how our spouse is spending money on sports tickets or buying a new television, and soon this becomes an outlet for venting our frustrations. It seems harmless, and it is easy to get the girls to agree that your guy is completely oblivious to your financial obligations. Everyone agrees with you that he needs his head examined. The problem about whining and complaining is that it will never help you solve any of your problems. Sure, it feels good to get the girls all worked up and on your side about the financial hardships that are not your fault, but it doesn't really address any of the issues. Sometimes, I think it is easier and more satisfying to keep whining and complaining, and become a victim, rather than address and resolve your problem head on. Don't get me wrong, a little sympathy from the girls is a good thing for a while, but sooner or later we need to get over it and move on toward solving the problems. Eventually, the girls are going to get sick of hearing about them.

Now for the fun part. In the chart below, write down all of your top complaints about money. This is your chance to whine and complain with complete abandon about all of the financial ruins in your life. Let's get it out of our systems, so that we can move on and start dealing with the real issues.

On the left-hand side of the chart, write down your ongoing, persistent complaints about money. These are the things you find yourself complaining to the girls about over and over again.

After you've made your list of complaints, use the right column to determine the underlying belief that is related to your complaint. Feel free to go back and reference your belief chart. This chart may also spark new beliefs, ones that you didn't realize you had. Typically, the complaint is just a symptom of a greater sickness, or in this case of the belief, which is below the surface, and causing the problem.

Persistent Complaint Ex: "My spouse is incompetent with money."	*The Underlying Belief* Ex: "It's a woman's job to take care of the money to run the household."

After you've made a list, take a look at what you've written down. These are some of your "Money Demons." These are the little toxic nightmares that will plague you every day of your life if you don't find a way to squash them every single time and place they pop up. If they go unchecked, they will prevent you from becoming financially successful. If you want to become a Rich Chick, we need to start the extermination process right now.

A true Rich Chick is not going to let the negative money beliefs she learned in childhood prevent her from getting what she wants out of life as an adult. So let's start practicing how we can rid these demons from our lives, forever. We're going to take the three toughest complaints you have about money and turn them upside down and inside out in order to create something positive that you will feel good about. In the space below, write down your three biggest money complaints—the ones that are constantly eating at you or dragging you down financially.

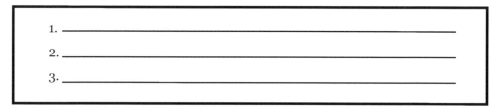

1. _____

2. _____

3. _____

Paying The Price

Holding on to these demons can take a toll on you. Take a closer look and see what your money demons are costing you. Here's a short list of some of the ways that your money demons could be having a negative impact in your life:

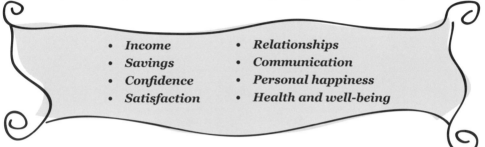

- *Income*
- *Savings*
- *Confidence*
- *Satisfaction*
- *Relationships*
- *Communication*
- *Personal happiness*
- *Health and well-being*

For each of the three money demons that you have written down above, write down the personal price that you are paying by hanging on to them.

Personal Price   *Demon 1:*
Personal Price   *Demon 2:*
Personal Price   *Demon 3:*

What You Get For Your Troubles

Guess what? Here's the flip side: You wouldn't be holding onto these costly complaints if you weren't getting some serious emotional juice out of them. Sorry, I hate to be the bearer of bad news, but that is how it works. We wouldn't continue hanging on to nasty complaints that cost us so much physically, financially and emotionally if we weren't getting something out of it. There are all kinds of emotional juices that come from these money demons. Plus, they give us the chance to feel helpless, so that our friends will sympathize with us, or feel sorry for us. That's powerful. I know it's hard to see and even harder to admit that a little tiny piece of us might actually be benefiting from these evil, little money demons, but believe it or not, it's possible to arrive at the place where we feed off of them and their negativity. On the other hand, by recognizing what we might get out of it and that it isn't all that good for us, we gain the freedom to choose their real worth. We have the power to stop wandering around like a helpless blob.

Here are some of the common things we gain from our Money Demons:

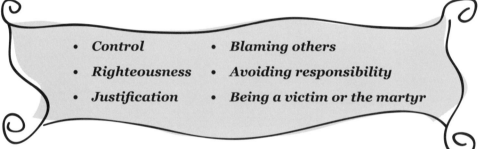

* *Control*
* *Righteousness*
* *Justification*
* *Blaming others*
* *Avoiding responsibility*
* *Being a victim or the martyr*

Take a real look at your Money Demons, and figure out what you are getting out of them. It might be difficult for you to nail it down at first; but in the end, it will be worth it to pin them down.

Emotional Gain   *Demon 1:*
Emotional Gain   *Demon 2:*
Emotional Gain   *Demon 3:*

Now that you can see what your demons are doing to you, don't you feel better? Once you know what your deceptive mind is up to, you can confront it and make a conscious choice about how you will deal with your money demons. Understand that it's possible to rid yourself of them forever.

Designing Your Destiny

Your beliefs about money influence your financial decisions. Each of these decisions will result in a particular type of outcome, and the results will determine your financial destiny. Basically, your money beliefs dictate your future, and if you leave them unchecked or ignored, you'll eventually lose control over your financial future. The good news is that it's possible to have total control over every situation. You have the power to decide how you are going to deal with these pesky little demons that are sucking the life out of your financial well-being. You are in charge, and it is time to take over the money demons that have been haunting you.

When it comes to money and finances, many people live their lives by the default beliefs they have put into place, never knowing that they could have made better choices and that they can access all the tools they'll need to change their financial future. Consider yourself lucky because you now know that you have ultimate control over your finances. You don't have to make financial decisions based on the rationalization or faulty childhood beliefs anymore. It's possible to discover new ways to view money and the world around you.

The Turnaround

All that is left for you to do is to kick those Money Demons out of your financial life. It's time to turn them upside down and make lemonade. It's as simple as turning your negative money beliefs into positive ones. It may be as simple as reversing your interpretation of a belief into something that makes you feel good and gives you more power. Take each of your Money Demons and flip them however you need to so that you can interpret them in a positive manner.

Typically, this means letting someone else off the hook, taking responsibility for something that you haven't owned in the past, or simply re-framing something that was holding you back. You'll be amazed how much easier and lighter your life can be when you toss the nasty negative money stuff in the trash.

Positive Belief 1: _____

Positive Belief 2: _____

Positive Belief 3: _____

Remember Angie? Though she didn't consciously go through this process, essentially, she took her old Money Demons that "it's the man's job to handle the money and finances" and flipped it so that she could do something positive for herself and her mother. Her new Positive Belief was that taking care of herself financially felt good! It gave her the confidence and satisfaction she needed to take charge of her life.

Now What?

With this newfound perspective on your negative money issues, you can positively change your future, and you can begin to act accordingly. Beliefs with no action are merely words or false promises. If you are going to become a Rich Chick, you've got to prove that you mean it. You have to do something that is going to move you forward into a brighter financial future. In the space provided, take time to write down one action step you can take for each new belief. It should be different from what you might have done in the past.

> **Positive Action 1:** _____
>
> **Positive Action 2:** _____
>
> **Positive Action 3:** _____

You have just done something most people will never do in a lifetime. You've faced some of your most personal beliefs about money, and those beliefs often cut to the core of who you are. This exercise is just the beginning of a lifelong journey of examining your choices about money and discovering more about the various things that influence those decisions. Money demons are crafty little creatures that will find new and sneaky ways to wreak havoc in your life. However, this process will give you the tools and structure needed to recognize them and squash them out. The possibilities are endless when you have the ability to make choices about money without relying on history, neglect or foolishness to make the decisions for you.

Defeating money demons will give you a clean slate so that you can free yourself and move on to becoming an ultimate Rich Chick. It's time to start figuring out your future, and that new day is just ahead of you.

Rich Chick Review:

Being *inquisitive* is the first step in becoming a Rich Chick. It will allow you to find out all kinds of things you never knew or realized about yourself. Unfortunately, some of your beliefs and values are negative, and they can cause money demons to take over and crush your financial future. Being inquisitive is about uncovering the truth and making positive choices about your resources and securing a healthy financial future.

Name three money demons that have been holding you back. (Fill in the blanks:)

_____

_____

_____

What are some of the positive changes you'll begin to make in regard to your financial future? (Fill in the blanks:)

_____

_____

How have the beliefs and values from your childhood influenced what you think about money?

_____

_____

What things would you do or say to instill positive money beliefs into your children or others? And, how have those specific things helped you?

_____

_____

Looking toward my Rich Chick future I will be more inquisitive by:

(Circle all that apply.)

- *Understanding that my childhood beliefs and values impact me today.*
- *Complain to all of my friends about how bad my financial situation is.*
- *Face money demons head-on and squash them out.*
- *Expect someone else to take the blame for my financial failures.*
- *Continue to uphold my values and beliefs, even if they negatively impact my financial future.*
- *I will not simply have beliefs, but will take positive action steps based on my beliefs.*

Rich Chick Tip:

Your beliefs and values are at the core of who you are, and you learned many of those beliefs and values as a child. As adults, we incorporate those ways into ideas that yield either positive or negative results. Being inquisitive means you can have total control over the decisions you make about your money. You can choose how you will deal with the Money Demons that haunt you, and evolve into a healthy lifestyle that will allow you to create fun and powerful ways to handle your money. Ultimately, the good decisions you make will positively impact your future.

Rich Chick Must-Have Accessory #1:

Inquisitive ☑

Chapter Two

"Finding your Flawless Canvas..."

Rich Chick Must-Have Accessory #2: Purpose

In finding your purpose as a Rich Chick, you have to be in this wholeheartedly. In order for all of the logic to pay off, and in order to reap the fullest benefits of becoming a Rich Chick, you must fulfill who you are, which goes far beyond your beliefs and values, or from simply having money. It's time to get your heart and your gut in the game too.

On my favorite makeover show, the make-up artist always says she's starting with a "flawless canvas." What she means is that if you make the bottom layer look perfect, or when you form a solid foundation to build upon, everything else will develop more naturally, and become even more beautiful than before.

Similarly, when you're talking about your financial goals, it's the foundation of those goals that sets the mood and pace for the results. What we're going to do in this chapter is uncover and refine your purpose and discover the foundation of your money makeover.

Obviously, you have an interest in having plenty of money at your disposal. Who doesn't want to be rich? Think of what you could do if you had an unlimited amount of money to spend. What would you do with it? The answer to that question is the key to the Rich Must-Have Accessory #2: Purpose. Read Barb's story below and you'll see that through a series of workshops she learned about her "True Purpose for Money." What's your "True Purpose for Money?"

Real-Life Rich Chick: Barb

Several years ago our company hosted a series of workshops for investors, which not only dealt with their money and investments, but the way that money affected the other areas of their lives. Each quarter we met with the same group of clients and covered new topics and tools related to money within each session. In one of the workshops, there was a couple named Barb and Tom, who had been clients for years. They were in their early 60's and had already retired. Barb had also been diagnosed with Lou Gehrig's disease and had less than one year to live. Yet, she came faithfully to her investor coaching classes.

One of the first exercises we did was called "Discovering Your True Purpose for Money." When we completed the exercise

Barb shared that her True Purpose for Money was "love." She wanted to use her money as a tool to express her love in the world, and to others around her. However, she also shared that she and her husband had a strained relationship with their children for years, but after delving into her True Purpose for Money, she now felt like the reason for their separation was over trivial matters. Before leaving the class Barb said she was planning to reconnect with her children and that she was going to share her True Purpose for Money with them.

Three months later, Barb came to the workshop in a wheelchair. Her health was obviously deteriorating; however, she was happier than she had ever been before. That night, Barb shared that she and Tom had re-established relationships with all of their children. They had invited them to visit, and they had reconnected and renewed each of their relationships. Barb was grateful to have discovered her True Purpose for Money, because in doing so, it motivated her and propelled her into action toward the thing she wanted most, which was to share her love with and for her children. Like Barb, each of us possesses the opportunity to discover our True Purpose for Money.

Most of us would love the luxury of having lots of money at our fingertips. I think most women, and men too, would like to be rich because of the opportunities that having money provides, but eventually, aimlessly spending wads of cash would become boring. There are only so many pairs of shoes one girl can wear, right? However, after you've bought everything you ever wanted, then what would you do with your money? It all comes down to your True Purpose for Money. That's what we are going to find out now.

Each of us has a belief system that underlies our decision-making process. Call it your conscience, moral compass or whatever you like. The point is that something guides you in making decisions about life. We all have a way of distinguishing right from wrong, and we all get a general feeling whether or not we should or shouldn't do something. We need to create that same kind of certainty around our financial decisions, so that our foundation becomes the flawless canvas upon which all of our decisions about money can be based.

Maybe I'm naïve, but I think that most people, especially women, are motivated by money for a variety of reasons, not just because of their own selfish desires. Most of us want to spend our money on the people we love and care about. We want to help the people we love so that they can lead better lives. That selfless motivation is the foundation of your "True Purpose for Money."

In the next few pages we are going to dig in and do some work. Like what we learned in the first chapter, these steps will give you a reason for becoming a Rich Chick. We're going to find out what makes you tick and why you value money. We'll discover why you are on this journey and how you'll be rewarded at the end.

Discovering Your True Purpose For Money

In order to reveal the things that are most important to you about money and wealth, we are going to start with the end result first. I'm going to ask you a question, which will take you many years into the future. Imagine yourself at a ripe old age, awaiting your peaceful and dignified death of natural causes, surrounded by your loved ones. Don't go getting depressed on me, in this version you have lived a very, very long and happy life and you are going out in style (and of course, you look fabulous). I'd like you to get there mentally, so you can reflect upon your life, your accomplishments and the legacy you'll leave. So, imagine yourself years from now, at the end of your life, and answer the following question:

"If I were at the end of my life, what would have to have happened financially for me to be able to say I have lived a life without regret?"

Typically, we don't think this way. We are too busy living in the moment, putting out fires, and managing ongoing chores that we are barely making it through the day. But taking time to think about our future for just a few minutes will have a tremendous impact on how we tackle money matters.

As you think about your answer to the question, here are a few things to consider:

- *Who are the people who are most important to you, including your family and friends?*
- *Are there any causes or charities that are important to you, where you would like to give and make a difference?*
- *Is providing education to anyone important to you, including your children or grandchildren?*
- *When would you like to retire? What would you like your standard of living to be at retirement?*
- *What kind of things do you want to surround yourself with cars, toys, jewelry, etc?*
- *What kind of experiences and adventures would you like to have throughout your life?*
- *Would you like to travel? Where to and how?*
- *How is your health and that of your family?*
- *Do you own property? Where? How much is it worth?*
- *Do you have any hobbies or interests that you would like to pursue?*

In the space below, I want you to answer the question. Take some time in your own private writing space to write down your thoughts and feelings. Grab your favorite pen and scribble away. Write down your goals as they relate to money and your financial outlook. Concentrate on the things you want to accomplish by the end of your life.

It is also important that you don't limit yourself in this process. You are not committed to anything by writing down your thoughts and feelings. Look at this as a wish list for how you would imagine or hope that your life would be fulfilled. Go for it. Don't deprive yourself of any of the luxuries in your imagination, and turn off rational thinking for a minute. Have fun with it.

"If I were at the end of my life, what would have to happen finacially for me to be able to say I have lived a life without regret?"
1.
2.
3.
4.
5.
6.
7.

Well, you did it. You wrote down your thoughts and dreams and answered one of the most important questions you'll ever be asked about your ultimate purpose in life. How do you feel? Did you know that you had all of those big plans? As women, it's in our nature to be giving—to our families and friends and to those we love. So in writing down your thoughts, you probably included others on your list. Love is one of the most motivating factors, and it can help us accomplish some of our biggest goals and dreams, even those that revolve around money. This chapter acknowledges that there is power in our purpose, and that gives us the drive to keep moving forward.

Each one of your goals reflects a specific value that you hold very close to your heart. So, we are going to take the next step and break down your goals into the "Why?" and discover what's really motivating you. So, the next question you need to ask yourself is this:

"What are the underlying values and priorities that each of my life goals represent?"

In the next section, identify a value that each of the goals you wrote on page 45 represents for you. List 7-12 value words that come to mind when you look at your goals.

Value Words

Here are a few words to get your creativity going:

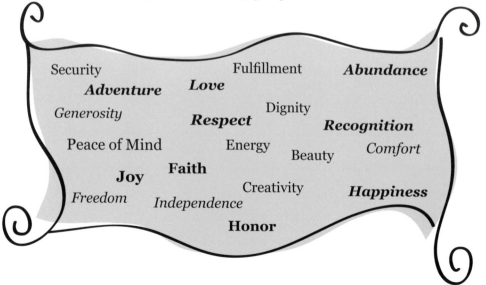

Security   Fulfillment *Abundance*

Adventure *Love*

Generosity   Dignity

   Respect   **Recognition**

Peace of Mind Energy *Comfort*

      Beauty

Joy **Faith**

     Creativity **Happiness**

Freedom *Independence*

   Honor

> ### *"What are the underlying values that each one of my goals represent?"*

1.
2.
3.
4.
5.
6.
7.

After answering several important questions, and by completing the previous exercises, you should not only have a list of goals, but a list of value words, or qualities of life—those that are most important to you. The next step we are going to take is to prioritize those values. Read over all of your value words, choose the top three and circle them.

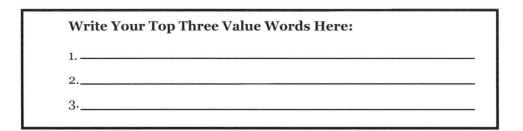

Write Your Top Three Value Words Here:

1. _____

2. _____

3. _____

Now we are going to do something even more challenging. Of the top three, carefully consider which one is the biggest, most important value. Try not to think of this as eliminating values, but rather as a summary of which one value encompasses all of the rest. Say it out loud, so that you can try it on like a dress. In doing so, you'll find that some look better on the hanger, and others look better on someone else. To make sure that your value word fits you perfectly, it should feel good to you when you think about it or when you say it. Once you've determined which one is at the top of your list, put a huge star next to the most important value word you choose.

In defining your purpose, ask yourself one final question. It's the final piece of the True Purpose for Money puzzle. Let's fast forward again, looking toward the mature adult years in your life and ask yourself one more question. Picture yourself there, knowing that you have accomplished all of the goals that you laid out, having expressed your values through your achievements. Now, in one word answer this question:

"How Do I feel?"

Which word best describes how you hope to feel? What would it mean for you if you accomplished everything you set out to do; everything you wanted financially, and in turn, you had the opportunity to express your values in doing so, living your life to the fullest? Do you feel peaceful, confident and secure? You decide.

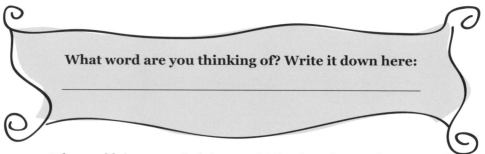

What word are you thinking of? Write it down here:

_____

Who wouldn't want to feel that way? Who doesn't want that sense of satisfaction that results from accomplishing all of their goals? This realization will also help you to define your ultimate purpose. Pursuing that goal is exactly what will keep you on the right track when it comes to making financial decisions. Now that we've defined our purpose, there is one last step in uncovering your True Purpose for Money and putting it all into one succinct summary.

Now, we're going to pull everything together into one comprehensive statement, which best expresses your values in an empowering way. The easiest way to do this is to start simple. Take your one value word and put it at the end of this sentence: "My True Purpose for Money is (insert your value word here)." You could make it more involved than that, but it's not necessary for it to become a complicated process. Let's see how it fits. Does it express your purpose? Is it what drives your goals and why you want to become financially independent?

If it's not quite there yet, feel free to refine it until it feels right. Spend the time you need to express yourself in the best manner possible. Don't get carried away; it's not rocket science and it doesn't have to be a novel. Honestly, if you try too hard to add too much to it, it will become watered down and less punchy.

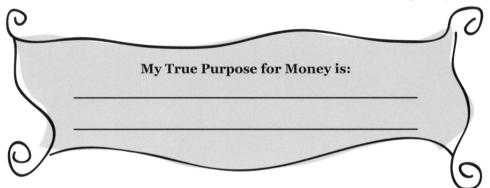

My True Purpose for Money is:

The greatest thing about having identified your True Purpose for Money is that it's not about the amount of money you have or will have; it's about making choices that are consistent with your purpose in life. Having a firm grasp on what you're made of and how you are going to use money as a tool to make things happen will help clarify many of your financial decisions.

My personal True Purpose for Money is to create happiness. I know that might sound a little ironic, particularly considering the title of the next section, but it's true. For me, happiness is what life is all about: being happy and helping others be happy. In my mind, if you and the people around you are truly happy, nothing is impossible. The great thing is that happiness is not dependent upon money, it can be created in the most difficult circumstances. I know that sounds a little "power of positive thinking" – but it works.

As a useful tool, knowing my True Purpose for Money is to create happiness really does come in handy. Obviously, when it comes to spending money, it gives me a chance to evaluate if the expense will make me or someone else, and not just the salesperson happy. Have you ever bought something and then later felt guilty and nauseous about it? That feeling takes away from my happiness, but using my True Purpose for Money as a tool helps me make better decisions and avoid all of that buyer's remorse.

"Money Can't Buy You Happiness."

"Money can't buy you happiness." Who actually says that besides your mom? These are the people who either don't have any money and want to make themselves feel better about it, or people who have money and are miserable about everything else in their lives. It's a true statement. Money can buy you things on the outside, but it can't do anything for you internally, as far as creating a peace, or a genuine happiness deep down inside. Money can't fix people who are broken, or those who've never discovered their true purpose. It can't give you your True Purpose for Money. You have to find out what that is for yourself. However, as a result of knowing your purpose, money can do many wonderful things to help you live a full and satisfying life.

While I accept that money can't buy happiness, the truth is that not having money can bring about a world of stress and unhappiness. The lack of it can certainly create problems. Many married couples fight about money more than any other subject. When we don't have money it can bring about stressful situations such as putting us in a position where we are unable to pay our bills. In reality, not having money is stressful and scary, and it limits our ability to create opportunities. So, let's keep going on this journey toward financial independence and toward "happily ever after" as we strive to live out life's purpose and our True Purpose for Money.

The True Purpose for Money goes far beyond acquiring a bunch of toys, an expensive house and nice clothes, or the general idea of being rich just so you can say you have money. It's about who you are. Money is a good and powerful resource if we keep our lives in balance and keep our financial concerns and motivation within a proper perspective. Purpose is about having goals and reasons for what you do with your money. It's about making life better for you and for others. With purpose, money relates to everything you are and what you are about.

Rich Chick Review:

My number one value word is _____.

My values represent my goals in these ways:

_____

_____

_____

_____

When it comes to understanding my true purpose, I should take these various things into consideration. (***Circle all that apply.***)

- *I want to be able to send my children to college.*
- *I don't need to worry about how much money I'll have after I retire.*
- *I want to travel and experience life's adventures.*
- *I'll have time later to explore my hobbies and interests.*
- *I want to own property.*
- *Worrying about my health is a waste of time, there's nothing I can do about it.*

In knowing my True Purpose for Money, I will set these three short-term goals, which I believe will greatly impact my financial future (fill in the blank):

_____

_____

_____

My current goals are different from those in my past because

_____

_____

_____

Rich Chick Tip:

Your True Purpose for Money is bigger than money – it's your true purpose for everything and what you are all about in life. Use it to motivate your best money decisions.

Rich Chick Must-Have Accessory #2:

Purpose ☑

Chapter 3

Have Your (Chocolate) Cake...

Rich Chick Must-Have Accessory #3: Future-Focused

Slaying the money demons and discovering your True Purpose for Money are crucial first steps on your Rich Chick journey. Now we're going to mix it up and have some fun finding your Future You. This is becoming *future-focused* on a grand scale. I'm not talking about setting weakling goals. I'm talking about setting big, scary, sassy goals that will get your blood pumping with fear and excitement. We're not only going to tackle goal setting in this chapter, but we will also design a plan for your entire future so that you will know exactly what you want to accomplish. This will help measure when you've arrived. And this is how you are going to have your cake, any flavor of your choice, and eat it too with Rich Chick Accessory #3: Future-Focused. Jessica is someone who was future-focused. Let's read her story and continue to explore what it means for each of us.

Real-Life Rich Chick: Jessica

Jessica was a 26-year-old paralegal who was stuck, or maybe she was just bored. Either way, she had been working at the same position in a notable law firm for 18 months and felt like she was going nowhere. While she didn't have any real complaints about her company or boss, she didn't see any potential for growth in her position, or anticipate any significant increase in her income.

In college, she dreamed of going to law school, but with college loans to pay back and not being a great test-taker, she opted to use her present degree and skills to help her get into the workforce, so that she could get on with her life. But now she wonders if she made the right choice.

One day, while leafing through a magazine and fantasizing about an imaginary life that would have taken her down a different track, Jessica started a project that she thought was silly at the time. She started writing down all of the things that she wanted, starting with things that she thought were silly and frivolous like shoes, purses and clothes; but then began taking it more seriously and imagined how she wanted her life to be.

She thought about her career and her desires; she thought

about her income and how much she wanted to make in the next five years; she thought about her health and her social life, and the kind of relationship she wanted to be in. For fun, she hung her list of things she'd written down on her refrigerator. Her friends commented occasionally, making fun of her plans and dreams, but she kept her list there—and it made her feel good.

Time passed, and her list eventually became part of the landscape of her kitchen. She never moved it. Then after about two years, she was moving and packing up her kitchen, and removed it from her refrigerator. Looking over the list, she was amazed at how many of her goals she had accomplished.

She was finishing up her first year of law school, moving in with her fiancé, and was ready to start the career she had always dreamed of. Her list had been the catalyst to amazing changes in her life. She tucked the list into her box of kitchen tools and planned to make a new one once she was settled into her new home.

As we look at what it means to be future-focused, we are not going to be vague in setting goals. We will set very specific milestones and vivid images to create your future. Your future plan is going to be customized just for you so that you will be able to incorporate all of your hopes, dreams and aspirations into a complete picture that expresses where you want to be in your life within a given time frame.

This will be so easy for you, because it's about focused daydreaming. I will begin by prompting you to think about various aspects of your life. Then you will use your imagination, with a little bit of reality in the mix, to create a five-year Future You that is compelling to you. This exercise is going to keep you excited and motivated enough to rearrange your life and achieve your financial goals. Remember that it's okay to stretch your imagination. Your possibilities are unlimited in the next five years. In order to accomplish your goals, you need to imagine the things that will challenge you to work harder, or at least differently, than you have ever worked in the past. You are only limited by your imagination and fear of the unknown. Knowing exactly how you will achieve your future goals is not imperative at this time. The most important thing now is your strong commitment to Rich Chick Must Have Accessory #3: Future-Focused, and that means having future-focused thinking.

First, find a comfortable chair, put on some comfy clothes, grab a tasty beverage of choice and relax for the focused daydreaming that we are about to do. Let's pretend there's a time warp and we've landed five years into the future. Everything we do from here until the moment I tell you to return from the future to the present is going to take place exactly five years from today's date.

Write today's date here (month, day, year):

_____

Write your Future You date here (month, day, year):

_____

In order to create a Future You that you can use on a daily basis, we're going to concentrate on five specific areas of your life. It will not only inspire you, but it will allow you to make the choices that will help you achieve your wildest dreams. By keeping your Future You at the forefront of your thinking, you'll feel great every day as you make the best financial decisions possible.

Financial

Let's get warmed up. The first area we will focus on is your financial outlook. I want you to envision yourself five years from today and answer the questions below.

How old are you (remember, it's five years from now... ouch)?

_____

What is your annual income?

_____

How much money do you have in your retirement plan?

_____

How much do you have in your personal savings?

_____

How much debt do you owe?

_____

Relationships

Who are the most important people in your life? What kind of activities do you share together? Where are your favorite places to spend time together?

_____

_____

_____

Professional Accomplishment

Think about your career. It doesn't matter if you are a professional or a stay-at-home wife and mother, or a top, corporate executive; think about the qualities of your work life, what it is like, and how it makes you feel. Then, describe your accomplishments below:

_____

_____

_____

Personal Fulfillment

What do you need personally to feel good about where you are in life? What does your personal life look like? What makes you happy? Think about the hobbies that you want to explore and the adventures you long to take.

What is your hair like?

_____

What kind of clothes do you have?

_____

What kind of books do you read?

_____

What time do you get out of bed on the weekends?

_____

What kinds of things bring you the most satisfaction?

_____

Where's one place you'd like to travel to?

Emotional Vitality

How is your health both physically and mentally? What do you do that makes you feel good? What new challenges excite you and make you eager to get up every day?

_____

_____

_____

_____

Okay, it's time for you to return to the present now. How did that feel? Did you let your imagination do the work and create a picture of your future five years from now? Hopefully, you are excited about what you have created; if not, try it again. There are no right or wrong answers; the only thing that matters is that you feel good about what you thought about and wrote down, and you have the desire to make it happen. It's okay to be intimidated by the _future you_ and it's okay to feel a little uncertain about how you are going to become her.

Now let's map out your five-year _future you_ and what you'll need to accomplish within the next five years, and then take a look at what's in between. In the space provided, continue looking at the same six areas of your life, but write down where you are today in each of these areas. Be totally honest. Don't worry about what other people might think. This exercise is for you. Sometimes I despise committing things to paper even if I'm the only one who will be reading them, because it makes them seem more like a reality. But trust me, this is the best way to outline the process. It's all for you, so it's best to be transparent about your thoughts and feelings. It's time for a reality check. We're going to compare where you are now to where you want to be in the future.

Future You!

	Today	5-Year Future You
What about your finances?		
How old are you?		
What is your annual income?		
How much money do you have in your retirement plan?		
How much do you have in your personal savings?		
How much debt do you owe?		
What about your relationships?		
What are your professional accomplishments?		
What is your personal fulfillment?		
What is your hair like?		
What kind of clothes do you have?		
What kind of books do you read?		
What time do you get out of bed on the weekends?		
What is your emotional vitality?		
What do you weigh?		
What is your exercise routine?		
How often do you exercise?		
What do you do for yourself that is indulgent for your emotions?		

As we map this out, you will start to see the differences between *future you* versus the person you are today. This is going to make it easier for you to begin to identify what you need to do in order to achieve your goals. Then we will begin to break it all down into achievable goals that you can set this week, this month and throughout the upcoming year that will begin to put your goals on track and into action.

When you look at the five-year *future you* compared to the current you, you'll see the areas that need to change and you'll be able to create a plan for each item on your list of goals. For example, if you want to double your income within five years, what will you need to accomplish between now and then to make that happen? Will you need to change careers? Will you need to move up the ladder at your current job?

As you begin to think in terms of what needs to happen in order for you to achieve your five-year goals, it will also be helpful to set a one-year, interim goal. This well help you define the changes you are committed to making in your life over the next year, and as a result, you'll be moving closer to your five-year *future you* goals. As you establish your one-year interim goals throughout the five-year period, you will be able to break each step or year down further in order to create a weekly or a monthly goal.

Don't forget to put a rewards system into place every time you reach one of your goals. It's important that you give yourself credit and acknowledge each of your accomplishments. I'm not talking about buying extravagant gifts for yourself, especially if you can't afford them, but you can reward yourself by finding a special treat, or with a night out on the town.

How Do You Like The Future You?

Congratulations! You have just done something most people in the world will never do...you threw your hat over the fence and made a wish that you can make come true. I know it can be a little scary to think that you just wrote down your most important and personal goals on paper, but that's okay. You have everything it takes to make your Future You happen and writing it down made it more likely to happen. Now you know what you're up to and what you have to accomplish. It will be so exciting to see yourself taking steps, leaps and bounds toward your goals.

Rich Chick Review:

What is the most exciting goal that you created in your Future You map?

_____

_____

What is the most surprising thing that you learned about yourself from your Future You?

_____

_____

What is the scariest thing you put on your Future You map?

_____

_____

Where are you going to hang your Future You map so that you can see it every day?

_____

_____

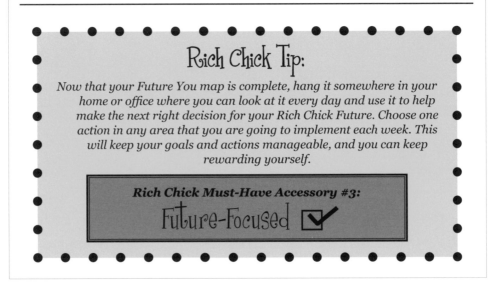

Rich Chick Tip:

Now that your Future You map is complete, hang it somewhere in your home or office where you can look at it every day and use it to help make the next right decision for your Rich Chick Future. Choose one action in any area that you are going to implement each week. This will keep your goals and actions manageable, and you can keep rewarding yourself.

Rich Chick Must-Have Accessory #3:

Future-Focused ☑

Chapter Four

Rich Chicks Come In All Shapes And Sizes

Rich Chick Must-Have Accessory #4: Determination

Now that we've talked about our beliefs, values and purpose, we can take our Rich Chick agenda a step further and move toward our determination. It's the Rich Chick accessory that will keep us moving forward into action. Along with discovering more about determination in this chapter, we'll talk about the different types of Rich Chicks—Single, Working, Married, Suddenly Single and Late-Blooming Rich Chicks. Before we begin to invest, we need to think about managing our money effectively, and this chapter will touch on that, too. Get ready for results as we dive into Rich Chick Must-Have

Accessory #4: Determination. If you're like me, you'll find different things bring about determination. Even in the midst of setbacks, challenges and failures, determination is a key accessory, one that will help keep us on track. Let's take a look at Susan's story and we'll see how her determination worked for her.

Real-Life Rich Chick: Susan

After 8 years of marriage, Susan's husband left her. She had two kids, a full-time job and a mortgage she would have to manage on her own. Life had thrown her a curveball that she never could have predicted. She was on her own and had to figure out what to do with her life, family, career and her money.

Susan was lucky that she had a supportive family, but she was also too proud to accept much help. At the same time, she was determined to make a good life for herself and her children. It took time, and the first years of being a single parent were not easy. They had to be frugal. Her children didn't have name brand clothes like their friends had and they didn't eat out at restaurants often, but they were happy. They took the resources they had and made it all work financially.

With focused planning and attention to her finances, Susan provided not only a good life for herself and her children, but she was able to prepare for her future as well. She put away money for her retirement, and saved a little to help each of her children attend college. It wasn't the full-ride college tuition that she had once hoped to provide for them, but it was enough, and they learned as much from their financial challenges as she did. Eventually, Susan's children learned to appreciate her efforts and realized her huge accomplishment.

Now at 48, Susan is enjoying the fruits of her labor, even though she once had to struggle. She is happily remarried, her kids are making their way in the world on their own and, though it wasn't the easiest path, she doesn't have any regrets. She can honestly say that her life is rich.

◎◎◎

Merriam Webster's Dictionary defines determination as, "the act of deciding definitely and firmly; *also*: the result of such an act of decision: firm or fixed intention to achieve a desired end —a woman of great courage and *determination*." *

With that in mind, let's think of determination as the thing that will single-handedly take us farther than any other Rich Chick Must-Have Accessory. Put on some jazzy music, and buckle into your favorite fashion belt, because the Rich Chick Must-Have Accessory #4: Determination is about to kick in.

No matter what kind of Rich Chick you are, you'll want to make sure you're determined, because it's that kind of stamina that will drive you throughout your Rich Chick journey.

While some people earn six figure incomes or salaries that go up into the multi-millions, the average person probably doesn't make hundreds of thousands, nor millions from their annual salary. That's why it's important to learn to live within your means, and to spend and save accordingly. Good money management skills don't happen overnight. That's why we need to be determined, and to go beyond the day-to-day and learn to look at how our choices will impact the bigger picture and what it could mean later on down the road. Say you splurge and spend $300 dollars and buy a couple of clothing items for yourself. That is probably okay if you do that once every six months or annually, or every couple of months, depending on your budget and your needs. But, if you spent that kind of money every week, it would begin making a huge dent in your overall financial situation.

I've learned from coaching others that good money management gives you the determination you need to go further with your financial priorities and investment skills. Once the money management aspect is in check, you can move on to other areas, such as investing.

What Kind Of Rich Chick Are You?

The Single, Working Rich Chick

When you're a single, working chick with no children to support, your excuses for not saving money should be limited. You don't have the demands of a husband and children, and all of the added expenses that come with having a family. Being single is the perfect time to invest in your future, providing you with the opportunity to invest some of that extra money you are making. It's important to take care of yourself financially. You owe it to yourself to become informed, savvy and wise about your investment options.

My friend Jennifer, whom I have known since high school, has worked for the same large company for the past 12 years. She makes fantastic money, is super smart and participates in her company sponsored retirement plan. When it comes to her finances, she is doing a lot of the right things. Yet, sometimes she's still overwhelmed about how to best invest her money.

She *wants* to invest her money, and she knows that she *should* invest her money, but she doesn't know *where to begin.* For years I've stumbled around trying to explain to her exactly how I invest my money, and I've tried to give her advice about how she can make right choices with her finances. Yet, there are still challenges and obstacles she needs to overcome when it comes to making wise decisions about investing.

We'll delve into the topic of saving more in one of the upcoming chapters, but everyone should be saving at least ten to fifteen percent of their gross income by investing it. A single, working chick should be saving even more. Chances are you won't be single indefinitely, and the older you are and the more lifestyle changes you experience, the harder it will be to save money.

One of the first places to look is at what kind retirement plan your employer has to offer. Find out what kind of underlying investment options are available within the plan, and if they follow the rules of investing and the accessories we'll cover in future chapters. Not all plans offer globally diversified, passively managed options. So, you need to take a close look at what is available, consider the options, and make your choices accordingly.

Even if you maximize your company sponsored retirement plan, you may still be eligible to contribute more money to an IRA or a Roth IRA. If not, you can always invest personal assets in a regular taxable investment account. If you are single, it is important to draft a will and coordinate beneficiaries on all of your retirement plans, because if you are saving money, you will want to make sure that if something unforeseen happens to you, your money and investments will be distributed they way you want them to be.

Becoming a Rich Chick now will provide you the opportunity of a lifetime to accomplish great things in your future. It will help you feel good about your finances both now and in the future. Don't let the opportunity to start investing early and the opportunity to build good habits now slip through your fingertips.

The Married With Children Rich Chick...

Welcome to the new millennium ladies. This is not 1950, and you are not June Cleaver. It's to your advantage to become knowledgeable and experienced when it comes to spending, saving and investing your money. It doesn't matter if you have a career outside the home or are brave enough to stay at home. Being in a marriage means you are in a long-lasting relationship with your mate. And that includes all of the different financial aspects as well. In order to work toward your financial future, you must work together as a team.

If you are a stay-at-home wife and/or mother, that doesn't automatically give you a free ride, or a lack of responsibility when it comes to taking an interest in your family's finances. If you are married, it takes teamwork. You and your husband will need to take the time and effort to communicate about money to make sure you are on the same page. In any relationship it's easy to become unbalanced by letting one person make all of the financial decisions, but it takes the commitment and ideas of both individuals to maximize ideas and opportunities. Couples often argue about money, because the scale is often out of balance.

With many couples, if the financial responsibility falls too heavily in one direction, it is often reflected within their bank account. When money comes down to a power struggle between a husband and wife, it will place a strain on the marriage.

You need to determine if you both have the same future goals for your money, and how you are going to go about accomplishing them. There are a couple of questions that can help you define your financial goals as a team: "Do your True Purposes compliment one another?" "Do you have common beliefs about how the market works?" "Do your Future Views line up?" "Are your Money Demons beating each other up, either figuratively or mentally?" Regardless of your goals, an Investor Coach can be very helpful for you. Investor Coaches are experienced in navigating through the various questions you'll face, and they'll ultimately help you get your money Mojo on track.

Whether or not you are both working, you can both have a retirement account in your individual names. This can be done through employer-offered plans or IRAs, but whatever options you choose, you need to make sure that everyone involved is taken care of in the future. If you are aggressive savers and want additional investments, you can always put them into your joint names so that you can continue to work together toward your common financial goals.

We talked about the importance of having a budget or some other measure of keeping your finances in check. The bottom line is that it's imperative that you both have a sense of your spending and saving habits. Establishing and maintaining a budget can be as elaborate as sitting down and spelling out everything with your monthly expenses to the dime, or something as simple as a plan that says, "We pay the bills first, then we see what's left." As long as you are not spending more than you are bringing in the door, you can come up with a budgeting plan that works.

Also, remember that it is important to have common expectations for the type of lifestyle that you can afford. You both need to be aware of what's appropriate for your income and what's within your financial means. Unfortunately, $1,200 handbags and $2,000 watches are not in most people's budgets; however, that same money could go a long way toward funding an IRA or investment account.

Another area relating to saving and spending is the amount of debt you owe. It's important to be aware of your debts and to have a plan and timeline of how you are going to pay them off. Whether it's student or car loans, or credit card debt or mortgages, your debt will accumulate quickly if you don't keep it under control.

Are We Saving Enough?

"Are we saving enough?" is another big question you'll need to address. The answer depends on how much money you are going to need to achieve your goals and when you'll need that money. This is another area of your finances where an Investor Coach can provide you with solid guidance and advice.

An Investor Coach will be able to guide you in not only finding the right investment vehicles for you, but also help ensure that your investments are appropriately protected.

Insurance

I know that it's unpleasant to think about an untimely death, but because we live in a random and unpredictable world, no one is immune to life's circumstances. If you provide for a family, insurance is another source of protection that can provide for those you love in a time of need.

The purpose of insurance is to protect your family from financial hardship in the event of death or disability. Generally, it is a good idea to insure all of your assets and income so that if something happens and you cannot provide for your heirs financially, your insurance will offset the financial responsibility.

In addition, you should also consider insuring any existing liabilities such as debts, your mortgage, and taxes. This would prevent the necessity of selling assets in order to settle your liabilities in the event of debilitating circumstances.

As part of the bigger Rich Chick picture it is important that you plan for the worst-case scenario, insurance is a part of that plan. Talk to an Investor Coach or insurance professional to determine if you have the appropriate kind and amount of insurance coverage for medical, death, and disability.

Wills

Whether you are single or married, it's important to have a will. Focusing your finances on your spouse and children is the only way to continue to provide for them, in the case of an untimely death. Preparing a will is the responsible thing to do in case something happens to you in the future. By not designating a guardian for your children in your will, you will make the trauma of their loss more dramatic with custody battles, and cause extended upheaval into their lives. In addition to their financial security and the relieved burdens that might arise, you'll also be taking other precautions when you name a potential guardian.

Building a Rich Chick portfolio means you will have assets or money that you want to designate to someone in the case of your death. If you die and are married and don't have a will, it would likely/automatically go to your spouse, if you don't specify otherwise. If you have any other family situation without a will, your money could possibly be tied up in the court system for years, with multiple people trying to claim it. Don't leave your loved ones in the lurch. It's best to plan ahead, even if it's a little bizarre and depressing to think about it right now.

Beneficiaries

Keep in mind that retirement and annuity accounts such as IRAs, 401(k)s, and 403(b)s have beneficiaries designated individually. Make sure that the beneficiaries on these accounts are coordinated appropriately with your other legal documents.

Suddenly Single Rich Chick

In addition to being single or married, there are other scenarios to think about. Sometimes the unpredictable happens in life and we find ourselves in an unexpected situation. One day, some of us Rich Chicks might find ourselves suddenly single by divorce or by death. During those times, it is more important than ever to have your financial picture outlined and accounted for so that you can take the appropriate steps to secure and maintain your positive financial outlook.

To be suddenly plunged into a single-again situation may cause you to feel lost and alone. If you're someone who hasn't been an active participant in your financial affairs up to this point, you may not only be in for some surprises, but you'll also be left wondering about your security and survival. If you don't know what's going on, it can be a long, drawn out process for you to take the time and energy to put all of the pieces of your financial puzzle together. But if you've kept up with your financial situation all along, it will be easier to respond when things come up.

You are going to need to get an accurate picture of your sources of income, and a projection of where your income will come from. Questions you'll have to answer if you're suddenly single will revolve around things like, "Will you be working and supporting yourself?" or "Do you have money coming in from an inheritance or spousal support?" It's best to have a plan, because your life can change dramatically overnight. And these changes can impact your lifestyle to varying degrees financially. Being prepared ahead of time will help you cope and become prepared for some of the challenges you'll face.

This is another time in your life where the support of a financial professional will be very helpful in sorting out all of the logistics that you'll have to manage. An Investor Coach can help you get on the right track and provide you with the information you will need to feel confident about the details and the future of your financial situation. When it comes to confiding in a coach, you'll need someone you can trust and feel confident in to help you through these difficult transitions.

The Late-Blooming Rich Chick

My mother has worked since she was 15 years old. She worked part-time at a local grocery store chain for 25 years. When she finally "retired" from there, she was honored with a lapel pin, which recognized her for all of those loyal years of service, but that kind of recognition wasn't going to help her financially. It didn't give her any kind of financial security for her future. When I was 12 years old, she became the first female firefighter in our small-town community. She worked part time, if you call 50 hours a week plus two night jobs as a firefighter/EMT/paramedic for 10 years, part time. Again, in this situation, she had nothing to show for her work in the way of retirement or long-term investment.

She put all of her blood, sweat and tears in for 30 years, but she had nothing to show for it in the way of investments or as a financial safety net for her future. But at 50 years old, she came to work at my office, where she was able to participate in a retirement plan for the first time in her life. Unfortunately, my mom is never going to become a millionaire, as much as I wish I could magically make that happen, but within the eight years that she has participated in the company 401(k), she has accumulated $100,000, which will continue to keep growing. She has also learned a lot about the investment industry and always says, "I wish I would have known then what I know now." Just imagine what kind of nest egg she would have built up if she would have invested in a 401(k) more than 30 years ago. From a financial perspective, my mom's situation is not all that different from 98 percent of all of the working and non-working women in our society. Maybe it's because she's my mom and I don't like to see her worry about money and the future, but this taught my mom and I both the value of good financial principles and investing in the future. In that same way, I hope to let every woman know that they have control over their Rich Chick future by taking the Rich Chick accessories to heart. You don't have to lie awake at night worrying about what you're going to do when you retire.

As my mom and I learned, it is never too late to learn about investing. It's feasible to continue being a stock market investor well into your retirement years. Many women in my mom's generation are concerned about how they are going to survive once they stop working. They have to face this reality head on. If you plan on maintaining your current lifestyle, you cannot count on social security to be your only source of income. As much as possible, you will need to plan ahead and save money to help you account for it. One of the biggest questions most women ask is, "Am I going to have enough money to retire?" Only you can answer that question, according to how you plan and what you do with the money you have at your disposal. It all depends on what you have done and are going to do to prepare for your retirement. Retirement is different for everyone, and ultimately depends on each person's expectations. But as a Rich Chick, you'll know the value of saving and investing your money wisely. Once you have clarity about your long-term goals and plans, you can take action and realistically come up with a solid budget. It may need to include other sources of income, beyond your personal savings or social security. But, as we already know, planning for the future and investing is the key to financial success. And investing as much as you can into your nest egg will ensure your success as a Rich Chick.

Rich Chick Review:

When it comes to your money, and what you're going to do with it, why do you think it is important to be determined? (Fill in the blank:)

_____

_____

_____

_____

What are some of the things that currently motivate you?

_____

_____

_____

_____

What goals will you set to keep you determined for the next week, month, year or five years?

_____

_____

_____

_____

What kind of Rich Chick are you? (Circle the choice that best describes you:)

Single   *Working*   *Married*

Suddenly Single   *Late–Blooming*

No matter what kind of Rich Chick you are, why is it important to be determined? How will that help you throughout your Rich Chick journey? (Fill in the blank:)

_____

_____

_____

_____

Why is it a good idea to have a will, and why is that important to you?

_____

_____

_____

Why does saving money matter?

_____

_____

_____

What can we learn from Jennifer and my mom? What things do you want to do that is similar to, or different from what they are doing/did in their stories?

_____

_____

_____

_____

List three things you are currently doing that help you effectively manage your money?

_____

_____

_____

_____

List three things you'll do in the future that will improve the way you manage your money?

_____

_____

_____

_____

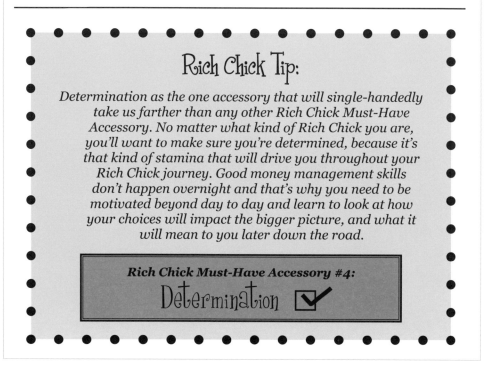

Rich Chick Tip:

Determination as the one accessory that will single-handedly take us farther than any other Rich Chick Must-Have Accessory. No matter what kind of Rich Chick you are, you'll want to make sure you're determined, because it's that kind of stamina that will drive you throughout your Rich Chick journey. Good money management skills don't happen overnight and that's why you need to be motivated beyond day to day and learn to look at how your choices will impact the bigger picture, and what it will mean to you later down the road.

Rich Chick Must-Have Accessory #4:

Determination ☑

Chapter Five

A Penny Saved Is A Penny Earned...

Rich Chick Must-Have Accessory #5: Discipline

No book about investing or getting rich would be complete if we didn't at least bring up the issues of spending, saving and that sometimes dirty word—budgeting. Rich Chick Must-Have Accessory #5: Discipline will teach you what you need to know most about budgeting, saving, spending and investing, and my favorite rule—pay yourself first. Read Carrie's story below and find out how her lack of discipline could have turned her world upside down. It isn't easy at times, but in the long run, it's the best way to go.

Completely Fictional Rich Chick: Carrie

To illustrate the accessory of Discipline and the concept of paying yourself first, instead of using a real-life example, I'm going to reference a well-known fictional character. Although I was never a devotee of the television show *Sex in the City*, I have caught enough episodes to become familiar with the characters, along with their individual circumstances and various traits.

Even assuming that magazine columnists, lawyers, and publicists in New York make obscene amounts of money, I was still amazed at how the SitC women could afford the expensive clothes and accessories they each wore. Not to mention the apartments they lived in, restaurants they frequented, and martinis they consumed.

In one particular episode, the main character, Carrie, is about to lose her apartment. In order to keep it, she has to buy it, but she has no money set aside for a down payment. While shopping for a new pair of shoes, which cost about $400, she realizes that she has about 100 pairs of shoes that cost an average of $400 each, which comes out to $40,000 in shoes. This is not what I mean by "paying yourself first." This example is the opposite of that principle.

To get out of this conundrum, two of Carrie's best friends offer to loan or give her the money for a down payment. Charlotte, who is independently wealthy, tells Carrie that it isn't her responsibility to bail her out and that she needs to be responsible for her own financial situation. Go Charlotte! However, in the end,

Charlotte gives Carrie her engagement ring from her ex-husband to sell, so that she can use the money to save her apartment. Not exactly a realistic ending to the story, but this is only television.

The moral of this story is to remind you to pay yourself first by taking care of your "needs" now and in the future before you begin spending money on your "wants." Most of us don't have friends with the money or inclination to bail us out of a situation like this.

When I first started working in the financial industry, one of the catch phrases that got thrown around a lot was "pay yourself first." There are many different ways you can interpret this phrase, but essentially what it means is to take care of your personal *needs,* financial and otherwise, before spending money on your wants. In the example above, our friend Carrie lived totally in the moment, spending the money she had on things that fulfilled her wants. Eventually, however, she came to realize and regret her indulgent spending habits.

I don't want this chapter to be a big lecture about arranging a structured budget. I think everyone is different and can find their own way to track and maintain their money. The bottom line is this: you have to live within your means and make more money than you spend. If writing it all down or managing it on your computer works for you, great—Go for it! There are many different budgeting tools and programs out there to help you.

Tips For Healthy Spending:

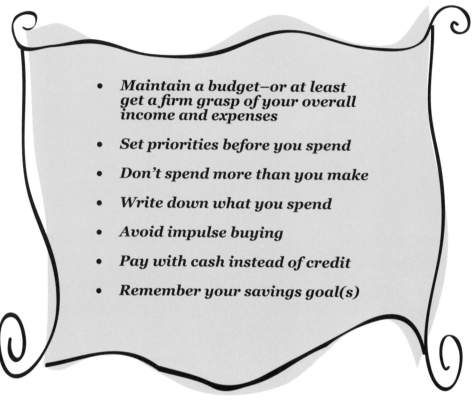

- *Maintain a budget—or at least get a firm grasp of your overall income and expenses*

- *Set priorities before you spend*

- *Don't spend more than you make*

- *Write down what you spend*

- *Avoid impulse buying*

- *Pay with cash instead of credit*

- *Remember your savings goal(s)*

What Kind Of Spender Are You?

Let's look at a couple of examples. If you are anything like me, sometimes you might need a little pick-me-up. And what that looks like in my life is a little "retail therapy." That's okay. Sometimes it's a trip to the local drugstore for some new lipstick or nail polish, and at other times it's off to the mall for clothes, shoes or a new purse. It depends on the kind of pick-me-up I need at the time. Whatever your "counselor" of choice is, remember that you are going to pay for it one way or another, either out of your checkbook or by racking up your credit card. If you are prone to this kind of therapy, I recommend having a fund set up in your budget that will cover these types of adventures. You can treat yourself to a luxury now and then, but make sure you include these kinds of expenses in your overall budget.

Quantity Or Quality: Watch Out For Spending Traps

Retail therapy might be one person's downfall, while bargain hunting might appeal to someone else.

By nature, some people are bargain hunters. If you are one of these gifted people, my hat goes off to you and I hope that you find amazing deals everywhere you go. If you are a bargain shopper, the one thing that you might want to watch out for while spending is buying things you don't need or things you want just because you find a great deal. I have seen my mom do this my whole life. My mother can find a bargain pretty much anywhere she goes. However, what I've noticed is that she has a closet packed full of clothes and shoes that she never wears. She has had clothes and shoes in her closet literally for years—with the tags still on them.

While the bargain hunter may not pay as much for an individual item as someone who shops at the front of the store, it is very easy to make up the difference in the amount spent in the quantity of bargain items bought. Forty dollars is forty dollars whether you spend it on four ten-dollar shirts or one forty-dollar shirt. Would you rather have one thing you love or four things to choose from? There is no right answer, except to only spend what you can afford.

Okay, so we've looked at the person who goes for retail therapy and we've also seen what bargain hunting looks like, but no matter what kind of spender you are, the most important thing is to have spending habits that fall within your budget. If you can't spare an extra four dollars for a coffee, or if you don't have an extra one hundred dollars for a trip to the mall, don't spend it. With that said, it is possible to have nice things that you enjoy and things that make you feel good, without overspending.

The Anti-Budget

Some people work well within a budget because the structure and limits that a budget provides establishes guidelines that help with spending and savings. Other people, myself included, do not work well within the confines of a budget in the strictest sense of the word. I have never been good about setting up a monthly budget plan, which allocates my financial resources to individual things. I think it's too much paperwork, too time consuming, and it requires a good deal of follow-up and energy to keep the budget updated and current. Blah, I can't take it. However, I have found that there are other tricks and creative ways to help control spending.

Here's one example. Several years ago, month after month, my husband and I kept running into the same problem—our checking account was overdrawn. My husband and I have a joint account, which we use for most of our day-to-day expenses, and we each have a debit card linked to that account. At that time, both of us were spending money without keeping track of it day-to-day and we ended up overspending. Even when I knew how much money we had in our account after all of the bills were paid, it still seemed like the money evaporated within minutes because we were both nickel and diming it to death.

But rather than cracking down hard with a complicated budget after our bills were paid each month, I took the majority of extra money out of our checking account and split the cash between us so that we each had our own share of spending money. That was the money we used to cover our daily expenses until the next pay period. This worked well for us for a long time. Utilizing the "cash plan" made me far more aware of how much money I was spending and how much I had left. When you have actual cash in your hands versus a piece of plastic, it can make a huge difference in regard to the things you choose to spend your money on.

If you're someone that has a habit of overspending, I realize old habits are hard to break. Overspending might feel good at that moment, but if you have been using retail therapy your entire life, it can keep you from getting ahead, or from becoming the best Rick Chick you can be.

It's important to remember that we all need a budget or a system that will keep our earnings and expenses in line with our spending and the amount we want to save, enabling us to live within our means. When spending is continually out of control, it has a tremendous negative impact on your financial future.

At the same time we set a budget, learn how much our expenses are and factor in what we will need to spend in the future, we should also focus on saving. Everyone has heard that old cliché, "A penny saved is a penny earned." What that means for us today is that if we save a little bit of money at a time, it could accumulate into a large amount of money in the future. And by saving a small percentage of your income, you could set yourself on the path to becoming a millionaire. Every Rich Chick needs a little bit of discipline to get there, and I'm going to show you how that discipline can help you save more than a penny.

Let Your Savings Work For You—The Beauty Of Compounding

Let's look at one example of how compounding works. Imagine that you bought a fantastic purse at your favorite store, but it's not in season, so you put it in your closet to use later. You forget about it. Then a year later while scouring your closet for items you want to take into the thrift store (which you can itemize and deduct), you find the purse, but now it's magically multiplied into two fabulous purses. Shocked and amazed, you leave them in the closet just to see what happens, and the next time you are rummaging through your closet, you find four purses. And every time you go back, the purses multiply by the number you have in there. That is the magic of compounding.

This is a completely figurative and unrealistic example. There is no investment that pays a one hundred percent return, and all investments carry risk. However, it makes the point that given the right circumstances, if you leave money alone, it can and will grow in incredible ways.

That concept works the same way when you save and invest money. Even when you save a relatively small amount of money, the return you earn on that money goes straight to the bottom line and is calculated into your future return. Similar to the purses in your closet, the longer you save money without dipping into your savings, the more money you will accumulate over time.

The Next Best Thing to Magic Is Compounding

When it comes to your money and financial independence, the concept of compounding can be magical. Compounding is when the money you make from an investment is reinvested to earn you more money than your initial investment. By reviewing the chart below, you'll be able to see the difference that saving one hundred dollars per month can make. In the scheme of things, a hundred dollars a month is a fairly small amount to save, yet it can earn you big money in the future.

Your Monthly Investment	Your Age	Total of Monthly Investments at Age 65	At 4% Rate of Return	At 7% Rate of Return	At 9% Rate of Return	At 12% Rate of Return
$100	25	48,000	118,590	264,012	471,643	1,188,242
	30	42,000	91,678	181,156	296,385	649,527
	40	30,000	51,584	81,480	112,953	189,764
	50	18,000	24,691	31,881	38,124	50,458
$150	25	72,000	177,294	393,722	702,198	1,764,716
	30	63,000	137,060	270,158	441,268	964,644
	40	45,000	77,119	121,511	168,168	281,827
	50	27,000	36,914	47,544	56,761	74,937
$200	25	96,000	237,180	528,025	943,286	2,376,484
	30	84,000	183,355	362,312	592,770	1,299,054
	40	60,000	103,169	162,959	225,906	379,527
	50	36,000	49,382	63,762	76,249	100,915

The earlier you start saving and investing, the better off you will be and the more wealth you will accumulate over time. It's never too late to begin, because every little bit counts, as every day counts until the day you take your money out of the market.

How can we take advantage of the magic of compounding? The first thing to do is start saving money. Many people don't feel that they can afford to save money. But asking yourself, "How can I afford not to save money?" puts an entirely new perspective on it. The sooner you begin planning for your retirement, the more prepared you'll become. It's the same mantra I've heard over and over again since I started working in the financial and investment industry, "pay yourself first." That doesn't mean buy yourself all kinds of frivolous things that you don't need before you give to charity. It means to first meet all of your basic needs by providing for yourself before you do anything else. Saving money is part of providing for yourself and your immediate dependents. Saving money is essential.

One of the easiest ways to "pay yourself first" is to invest money in a retirement plan. If you work for a company that provides a retirement plan like a 401(k) that is a good place to start. You can set your contribution amount to be taken directly out of your paycheck, before taxes. You won't pay taxes on retirement funds until you withdraw them out of your retirement account. One of things I like about a retirement plan is that it is not easy to withdraw the money, and that is a good thing, because you'll continue to accumulate more money. It is an ultimate fix-it-and-forget-it investment tool. The longer your money stays in the account, the more it will grow.

You might be thinking to yourself, "I live paycheck to paycheck and I can't afford to have any money taken out of my check." Let me give you a couple of things to think about. First, every little bit counts. As you can see from the compounding chart earlier in this chapter, it doesn't take a huge amount of money every month to build up to a nice nest egg. Secondly, as human beings we are amazingly adaptable and resourceful creatures and we can learn to live on what we have. For example, if the money you invested into your retirement account is no longer there to spend, you'll soon find other ways to make ends meet. You'll learn to cut back on small luxuries or find alternate sources of income to make up the difference.

One factor to keep in mind is there are limits to how much you can contribute to your retirement plan pre-tax. However, if you are contributing the maximum tax-deferred amount, you are stashing away a few thousand dollars a year toward retirement and that money will continue to grow and compound until you retire. If you have questions about what the current tax laws and limits are in retirement plans, talk to a tax professional.

Who Wants To Be A Millionaire?

Depending on how old you are and how much you are willing to stash away, becoming a millionaire is a reachable goal for many people. Here's what one typical situation might look like. My thirty-three-year-old friend Stephanie has nearly three hundred thousand dollars in her 401(k) plan and it doesn't seem to hurt her a bit financially. Some of the money is what she personally contributed, some is growth from her investments, and some is her employer's contribution to the plan. That money didn't seem real to her because although she worked for it by doing her job, she never noticed that she was saving it, nor how much she had saved. That is how the magic of retirement plans and compounding works. If we factor in the value of her home and personal property, she could become a millionaire before she turns thirty-five.

Saving money in this manner is a fairly easy habit to get into, because you don't have to physically do anything to make it happen. You can fund any kind of retirement (401(k), IRA, etc.) or savings account by setting up automatic withdrawal from your paycheck or from your bank account for direct deposit into your retirement account–that's it. Plus, once you start doing this, you'll start to see your money grow and it will feel good. Investing your money will become so exciting and fun, you won't want to stop saving.

Plus, there is icing on the cake. If Stephanie were to stop contributing to her retirement plan today (which she shouldn't do) and let it sit without touching it until she's eligible to take the benefits at age fifty-nine and a half, it would be worth over 2.3 million dollars, by keeping it invested at an eight percent rate of return. If she keeps contributing $5000 per year until retirement, at an eight percent rate of return it will grow to over 2.8 million dollars!

How Much Do I Need To Save?

As a general rule of thumb, you should save at least ten percent of what you make, annually. If you are making thirty thousand dollars per year, you should be putting at least three thousand dollars per year in some type of plan. That's two hundred and fifty dollars per month that you cannot spend on luxury items, such as clothes, shoes, purses, expensive coffee or eating out frequently. The more money you make, the more you should be saving, and the more you save, the better.

Getting It Done

Use the worksheet below to figure out how you can get started by "paying yourself first:"

What is your annual income? $_____

**x10 percent (how much you
need to save per year)** $_____

Divided by 12 months $_____/per month_____

Once you complete the above worksheet, you'll arrive at a monthly number. That is what you will need to save in order to get started on building your dream home or whatever it is you want in the future. You will have to be realistic about what kinds of things you can give up in order to accomplish your goals. Is it a four dollar cup of coffee or a four hundred dollar pair of shoes that you want to part with? It doesn't matter, but you will have to get creative with your spending in order to make saving a top priority.

Rich Chick Review:

Why is saving money essential?

_____

_____

As a general rule, how much money do I need to save? Annually and each month? (Fill in the blank:)

_____

_____

How does my budget look, and how does it compare to what I'm spending and saving?

_____

_____

_____

What does it mean to "pay yourself first?"

_____

_____

Briefly describe how compounding works?

_____

_____

Why is my company 401(k) plan a good idea?

_____

_____

_____

What are the differences between an IRA and a Roth IRA?

_____

_____

_____

Now, answer the following questions by checking "Yes" or "No."

I currently save at least 10 percent of my income	☐ Yes	☐ No
I contribute to my company's 401(k)	☐ Yes	☐ No
I pay with cash instead of credit	☐ Yes	☐ No
I have a budget and align my spending and saving accordingly	☐ Yes	☐ No
My expenses are in line with my income	☐ Yes	☐ No
I regularly set savings goals	☐ Yes	☐ No

If you answered "Yes" to four or more of the above, you're probably well on your way to becoming a Rich Chick. If you answered "No" to four or more of them, you need to work on being more disciplined with your money.

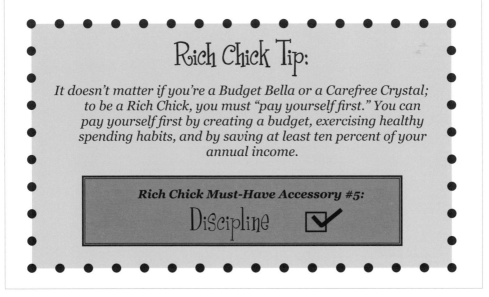

Rich Chick Tip:

It doesn't matter if you're a Budget Bella or a Carefree Crystal; to be a Rich Chick, you must "pay yourself first." You can pay yourself first by creating a budget, exercising healthy spending habits, and by saving at least ten percent of your annual income.

Rich Chick Must-Have Accessory #5:

Discipline ☑

Chapter Six

If A Tree Falls In the Forest and There Is No One There To Hear It...

Rich Chick Must-Have Accessory #6: Savvy

We've learned about discipline, and now we understand the power of what it means to pay yourself first. In this chapter, we'll learn how to do that by incorporating Rich Chick Must-Have Accessory #6: Savvy. In becoming a Savvy Rich Chick, this chapter will help you understand what options and investment vehicles are available to you and how you can best take advantage of them. Just because you're not hearing the proverbial tree fall, doesn't mean you shouldn't take the time and energy to find out what your investment options are. When it comes to your money, ignorance is not bliss. A Rich Chick is wise about her investment choices. Kim is someone who was a Savvy Rich Chick. Take a look at how just how her savvy worked.

Real-Life Rich Chick: Kim

Kim is a young wife and mother of three. She stayed home to raise her kids while her husband worked to support their family, and she was happy with her lifestyle. As a family, they were very careful with their finances; they kept their debt minimal and managed to save some money while maintaining an average, middle-class home.

As her children got older, Kim decided that it was time to go back to work. At age 35, she got a job with a growing investment management company as an administrative assistant and she quickly moved up within that small company.

Working with an investment company was a new experience for Kim. She had gotten an education because she had never before been exposed to the deeper aspects of investing and finances. Kim was aware that her husband had a retirement plan through his Fortune 500 company, but she never considered what she might need in the future.

Kim didn't know that the world of investments and retirement plans apply to everyone, not just to people who work for big organizations. The fact that she had no savings or retirement money to support her in her retirement years wouldn't have helped her down the road. If she hadn't discovered the importance of having her own retirement account, she possibly would have found herself in a difficult situation later in her life by solely depending on government income or her children to survive.

Luckily, Kim's savvy kicked in quickly once she was aware of what she needed to do, and she immediately started contributing as much as she could to her company's 401(k) plan. Now she has the great sense of satisfaction and confidence knowing that she will not have to rely on someone else to take care of her in the future. She is taking care of herself, her family and preparing for the future.

We've all probably made money mistakes in the past, but in becoming a Savvy Rich Chick, we'll no longer have to let our hard-earned money slip through our hands. So, let's dive in and take a look at some of the investment options available, how to make wise choices, and how we can make the most of our investment opportunities. Are you ready for your own Rich Chick adventure to begin? Let's get down and dirty about Rich Chick Must-Have Accessory #6: Savvy. Savvy is knowing what your options are and acting on them, ultimately paving your way to becoming a millionaire.

The first hurdle to clear when getting savvy is to identify which vehicles or "money holders" are appropriate and most beneficial to you. Basically, if you are saving ten percent of your income, you have to decide where you are going to put it.

The Most Common "Money Holders" Include:

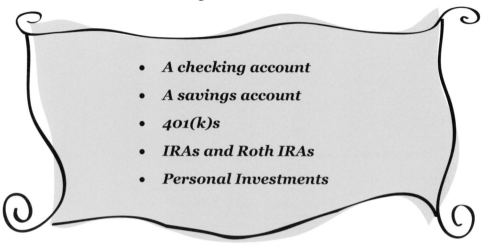

- *A checking account*
- *A savings account*
- *401(k)s*
- *IRAs and Roth IRAs*
- *Personal Investments*

There are advantages and disadvantages involved with each type of "money holder," but the end goal of each is to help you grow your money and help you make wise financial choices. The Rich Chick Method will help you become Savvy about investing. As a result, you'll become well-informed and gain a keen perception about your best options. Now, let's get your Rich Chick Savvy started by teaching you the basics, and by the end of your Rich Chick adventure, you will have more Rich Chick Savvy than you ever imagined possible.

"Money holders" like a checking or a savings account will help you lay the groundwork for responsible financial management. Once you've established that foundation, you can move on to other complex and potentially profitable investment options.

From my own experiences, I've found that investing is the way to go. A company retirement plan or IRA is a good place to start, because these type of plans have multiple benefits and it's a fairly easy way to begin to grow your money. When looking into options like 401(k)s, IRAs or Roth IRAs, the first thing you need to do is figure out what tax-deferred options are available to you, and invest there first. This means that you'll invest money now but won't pay taxes on it until you withdraw the money at retirement age.

Let's Take A Look at A Few Of The Investment Options To Consider:

401(k) Plans

First, if you're employed, find out if your company offers a retirement plan, which is typically a 401(k) plan. What's great about a 401(k) plan is that you can contribute to it directly from your paycheck. You never handle the money yourself, which reduces the temptation that you'll use the money for something else. All 401(k) plans are different, but many companies offer partial or matching contributions, which will help to grow your savings at an even faster rate. The limits on how much you can contribute to your 401(k) vary based on each individual plan. One of the fastest ways to build your financial nest egg is to maximize your contributions and take full advantage of the benefits that your particular 401(k) plan offers. If you're unsure about the various options your employer offers, check with your benefits administrator. With 401(k)s, you must be selective about the investments you choose within your plan, and we will cover those investment choice specifics in a later chapter.

IRAs

The second type of tax-deferred retirement plan is called an Individual Retirement Account (IRA). An IRA is an account that you fund independently, meaning you put your money in after taxes and then deduct the contribution when you file your taxes at the end of the year. You will still receive the same tax benefits as if you contributed before the taxes were withheld from your paycheck.

However, there are limits as to how much you can contribute to an IRA on an annual basis. Depending on your yearly income, you may be able to contribute to both your company sponsored 401(k) and an IRA.

Another IRA-related option is the Roth IRA. The Roth IRA is like a regular IRA, but instead of contributions being tax-deferred now, withdrawals are tax-deferred. The benefit here is that you pay the tax on it now and, theoretically, when you are older and in a higher tax bracket you won't pay the higher taxes on the money. Maximum contributions change from time to time, depending on your income and the tax laws. To obtain the current information regarding contributions to retirement plans, contact a tax professional.

What's Inside?

Once you've decided to utilize a retirement account, you'll need to find out more about what to put in it. It's not just a savings account where you'll receive a set interest rate and you can forget about it. Retirement accounts are designed so that you can benefit from being a stock market investor.

What Is Stock?

A share of stock is a piece of ownership in a particular company. Typically, there are two kinds of stock—common stock and preferred stock. Preferred stock is different from common stock because it doesn't carry voting rights, but it does allow the owner to receive dividend payments before these payments are issued to other shareholders. A shareholder is an individual or company who owns one or more shares of stock in a particular company. Investing in the stock market allows you to grow your money over the long-term at a higher rate than inflation, and it is fairly simple to become an investor.

A Deeper Look into the Market:

The "market" is the term used to describe the stock market in general. It is a collection of stocks issued by individual companies that are traded on an exchange. An exchange can be either a physical trading floor where people run around and shout out prices to trade stocks in person such as the New York Stock Exchange (NYSE), or an electronic exchange where all trading is done via phone or computer like the National Association of Securities Dealers Automated Quotation System (NASDAQ) or the American Stock Exchange (AMEX).

Who Reports On How the Market Is Doing?

Dow Jones Industrial Average (DJIA) – Also, commonly called the Dow or Dow Jones, the Dow Jones Industrial Average (DJIA) is one of several stock market indexes that measures how the stock market is doing, and primarily reports the performances of the industrial sector of the United States stock market. The DJIA is computed by using the stock prices of 30 of the largest and most widely held public companies in America.

Standard & Poor's (S&P 500) – The S&P 500 is a value weighted index of the prices of 500 large-cap, actively traded common stocks in the United States. Stocks included in the S&P 500 are large, publicly held companies that are traded in either the NYSE or the NASDAQ.

New York Stock Exchange – (NYSE) Based in New York City, with its trading floor on Wall Street, the New York Stock Exchange is the largest stock exchange in the world. Operated by NYSE Euronext, which was formed with the NYSE's merger with Euronext, affords a way for buyers and sellers to trade shares of stock in companies registered for public trading. For more information, visit www.nyse.com.

National Association of Securities Dealers Automated Quotation System − (NASDAQ) Exchange is done over a network of computers and telephones, and transactions are completed electronically. Established by the NASD, this computerized system facilitates trading by providing brokers and dealers with current bid and asking price quotes of various stocks. With the NASDAQ, there is not a physical trading floor that brings together buyers and sellers. For more information, visit www. NASDAQ.com.

How Does the Stock Market Work?

The stock market works based on the economic principle of supply and demand. That means the prices of the goods and services are determined by what the free market will pay for them. This concept applies to you whether you are buying groceries or investing in the stock market. The stock market is the greatest wealth creation tool known to womankind, and a Savvy Rich Chick takes advantage of all the market has to offer.

When the price of a stock falls or is "down," that means that there is more stock available on the market than people are willing to buy. The price is lower because there is more supply than there is demand. Alternately, when the price of a stock is up or "high," there is more demand for it than there is supply in the market and it is more expensive to acquire.

One or two people, or a group of people who are trading on Wall Street don't determine stock prices. Every single investor who owns stock and is participating in the market determines stock prices. Simply by owning investments in the stock market, you are participating in the system and are part of the collective group of people who are determining stock prices.

The biggest reason that stock prices seem so random and unpredictable is because they are random and unpredictable. The potential market is made up of over 6.7 billion people so it is impossible to predict how a particular stock is going to fare on any given day. Thankfully, this book does not rely on predictions about the future or the market to ensure Rich Chick results. Once you implement the ***Nine Rich Chick Must-Have Accessories***, you will have everything you need to place yourself on the path to becoming a millionaire.

Should I Invest In the Stock Market?

If you are under the age of 70, the answer is probably yes. If you are looking to grow your savings faster than inflation, which historically hovers just over three percent per year, your nest egg needs to grow at an average rate of more than three percent per year just to cover your cost of living. You must be invested in the market to achieve those kinds of results.

Though the stock market fluctuates, it is a powerful investment tool. There is no other tool that can help you build your wealth and financial independence as efficiently and effectively as the stock market. With a solid investment philosophy, grounded in proven economic theory and a realistic time horizon, you can grow your wealth exponentially.

Mutual Funds

Mutual funds are a great investment option. The easiest way for the average investor to invest in the market is through mutual funds. A mutual fund company takes the investment capital or the money from many different people, and uses it to buy different stocks, bonds, etc. to create a portfolio. Each person who buys shares of the mutual fund owns a portion of the overall portfolio.

In considering mutual funds, it's important to remember that all mutual funds are not created equal. A Savvy Rich Chick looks for low-cost, low-turnover, well-diversified funds that are passively managed; meaning the manager sticks with the same holdings and doesn't make changes based on predictions, assumptions or other futile attempts to beat the market. The reason this is a good idea is because we are not interested in trendy or hot investing. We are looking for a beneficial, long-term solution to our financial needs. Well-grounded investing lasts a lifetime.

The Market Offers Rewards and That Involves Taking Risks

Being invested in the market isn't like having a savings account. There is no free lunch when it comes to investing. To attain the biggest rewards that the market has to offer, you have to be willing to take on additional risks. Every investment has a certain amount of risk associated with it, but a Savvy Rich Chick takes that risk because we believe that the reward is worth it. For example, we invest emotionally in relationships at the risk of our happiness, because the rewards we receive from our relationships are much greater than the potential downside. Remember to take into consideration that there will be times when the market will decline, because there will be times when we need to sit back and wait for it to recover.

When it comes to investing your money, risk and reward should be related. The more risk, the greater the potential reward. Different types of investments carry different levels and types of "risks," but as a general rule you should only be taking risks that will result in rewards.

Becoming a long-term investor doesn't mean that you jump in and out of the stock market for a year or two. Building your portfolio is a life-long process. Your portfolio is going to have its ups and downs. Yet, if you select stocks and other investment options carefully, you'll weather the storms well and gain substantial wealth over time. When you select a long-term strategy for building your portfolio that is backed by sound economic principles, you will have created a long-term plan that will endure even through rough market conditions.

Sometimes A Frog Is Just A Frog...

Although investing is a long-term commitment, much like a relationship – not all portfolios or investments are created equal. It can be very hard to know if you are getting what you need inside your portfolio.

At times, investing can be compared to a frog and a prince. Of course, you always want to go for the prince. However, sometimes a frog is just a frog, and no matter how many times you kiss it, it's never going to turn into a prince. In the same way, if you end up with a portfolio or a frog that isn't made up of the right materials, no matter how long you stick with it, it may never yield the results you are looking for. That's why it's important for you to get a firm grip on all of the Rich Chick accessories so that you can use your newfound knowledge to find the right portfolio and an investment strategy that is best for you. Once you find the right portfolio, like the perfect prince, you will gain years of satisfaction and growth that you never imagined possible.

The Great Stabilizer – Fixed Income

At the other end of the spectrum from the stock market is what is called fixed income investments. These types of investments are considered less risky, but do not pay the same kind of return as the stock market. Fixed income investments play an important role in the portfolio as a stabilizer for equities.

Fixed income instruments include:

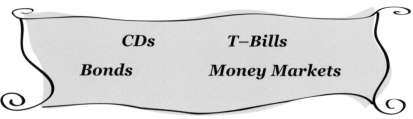

CDs　　*T–Bills*

Bonds　　*Money Markets*

CDs

The idea behind a certificate of deposit (CD) is that you lend your money to a bank for a specific amount of time, often up to five years. Then, you'll receive a certain amount of interest on the loan, and when the CD reaches maturity, you'll get your money back. The benefit to owning a CD is the amount of interest you'll earn, and that varies based on several factors, including the bank, the amount of money you lend or put into the CD, and the competitiveness of interest rates.

Money Markets

A money market is a mutual fund that aims to keep its share price consistently at one dollar. Money market funds are used by professional money managers to buy stocks, bonds and mutual funds. Like a checking or savings account, this is a simple investment tool, and the cash is readily available for alternate investments.

Bonds

Similar to CDs, bonds are a fixed income instrument in which the investor loans their money to the institution (government or corporate) for a defined period of time at a particular interest rate. Bonds can be either short-term or long-term, and interests rates vary based on the length of maturity.

T-Bills

T-Bills are short-term debt obligation investments, backed by the U.S. government. Unlike bonds, T-Bills have a maturity of one year or less.

Real Estate or Property

For most of us, investing in real estate boils down to owning a home.

Others take real estate investing a step further by investing in property, such as owning apartments or rental houses, land ownership or commercial property, and so on. When we purchase property, or anything of substantial value, we are making an investment. But when you start talking rental properties, etc. you're talking more about a job, where you have to maintain and manage, rather than an investment that does the heavy lifting for you while you go about your business.

We've learned that there are a number of different ways to invest your money, as you're getting your Savvy started, you should plan on participating in or opening some kind of retirement account. As your money grows, you should keep in mind that the highest long-term returns come from being a participant in the stock market. A Savvy Rich Chick understands the power of investing and is continually taking proactive steps to maximize her money.

Rich Chick Review:

A Savvy Rich Chick is someone who (define):

_____

_____

By becoming a Savvy Rich Chick I can (list the results):

_____

_____

I can become savvier by (list two or three things you are doing, or will start doing):

_____

_____

Savvy steps to take on my Rich Chick journey include:
(circle all those that apply):

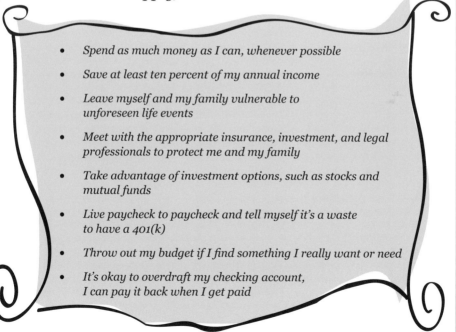

- *Spend as much money as I can, whenever possible*

- *Save at least ten percent of my annual income*

- *Leave myself and my family vulnerable to unforeseen life events*

- *Meet with the appropriate insurance, investment, and legal professionals to protect me and my family*

- *Take advantage of investment options, such as stocks and mutual funds*

- *Live paycheck to paycheck and tell myself it's a waste to have a 401(k)*

- *Throw out my budget if I find something I really want or need*

- *It's okay to overdraft my checking account, I can pay it back when I get paid*

Here's a list of the investments I currently have: (Make a list)

_____

_____

_____

_____

_____

Investments I'd like to make in the future include: (Make a list)

_____

_____

_____

_____

_____

I'll begin taking these practical steps in regard to Savvy investing:

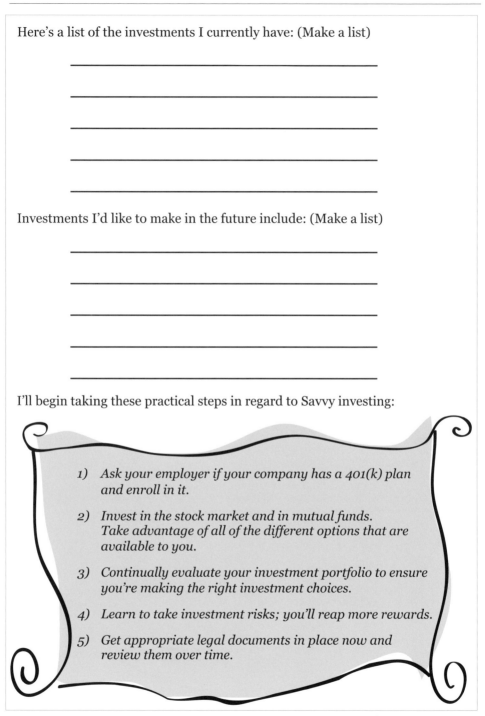

1) *Ask your employer if your company has a 401(k) plan and enroll in it.*

2) *Invest in the stock market and in mutual funds. Take advantage of all of the different options that are available to you.*

3) *Continually evaluate your investment portfolio to ensure you're making the right investment choices.*

4) *Learn to take investment risks; you'll reap more rewards.*

5) *Get appropriate legal documents in place now and review them over time.*

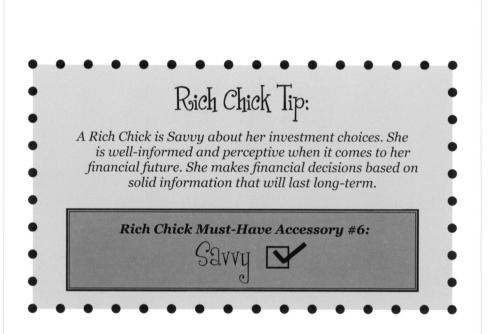

Rich Chick Tip:

A Rich Chick is Savvy about her investment choices. She is well-informed and perceptive when it comes to her financial future. She makes financial decisions based on solid information that will last long-term.

Rich Chick Must-Have Accessory #6:

Savvy ☑

Chapter Seven

It Doesn't Take A Rocket Scientist, but A Few Nobel Prize Winners Can't Hurt...

Rich Chick Must-Have Accessory #7: Intelligence

With the right information, you are smart and savvy enough to become a Rich Chick. It just takes a little bit of education and common sense to achieve it, which brings us to the next key principle we're going to explore—The Rich Chick Must-Have Accessory #7: Intelligence.

To become a successful investor, there are a few basic principles that you need to know. One reason women are good investors is because most women like to work within a plan and stick with it. Generally, women are patient and don't always need to make a change just for the sake of change. As women we are willing to ask for help and are inquisitive about the things we need to know. Sarah is one Rich Chick who let her Intelligence take her to the top. We can all be like Sarah and acquire the intelligence we need.

Real-Life Rich Chick: Sarah

Sarah is a professional who has been working in the same organization for ten years. She is very financially responsible, owns her home, lives comfortably within her means and is doing all the right things in regard to effectively managing her money. She has been participating in her company's retirement plan since she was first eligible and she feels good about what she is doing. Sarah knows that she needs to save for retirement and plans to retire young, so that she can enjoy the fruits of her labor.

While she is doing all the right things, Sarah still feels baffled by what happens within her retirement account. She chose investments for her 401(k) based on what options the benefits administrator told her were available, and based on the brief descriptions of each option. However, she doesn't understand why her account goes up and down the way it does.

Sarah considers herself a moderate risk taker and wants the benefits of being a stock market investor, but she doesn't want to risk everything, especially the money for her early retirement, by making bad investment decisions. Even though she was investing in a 401(k), Sarah felt like the information she was getting from her company plan wasn't in-depth enough to make educated decisions about what to do with her retirement funds.

After tolerating the frustration of not knowing what to do for a year or two, Sarah decided to ask a professional. She began attending financial seminars and workshops in her local community, and she finally found a financial advisor or an investment coach that she felt comfortable with.

Her coach spent time with her, asking Sarah important questions about what she wanted to accomplish with her money and offered ongoing education about investing and finances, which was exactly the kind of information Sarah was looking for.

After only a few weeks, Sarah had reevaluated what she was doing with her company retirement money and was able to establish another long-term investment account that would become available to her in her early retirement years. She now feels confident and secure about what she is doing with her financial future and is on her way to achieving her dreams.

Like Sarah, when it comes to matters of money and investing, one of the biggest challenges is that we don't always know where to go to find the proper information that we need. And more importantly, there's certain information and advice we should avoid. For now let's forget about investing related television programs, radio shows and magazines. Many of them are filled with futile information or packed with advertising schemes that we don't need. They might try to hook us with fear or anxiety or try to distract us with the latest market trends in the world. The most important thing to remember is to keep focused on building and strengthening our portfolios long-term.

When it comes to investing, our confidence and peace of mind should revolve around the components of our portfolios. Because of our patience, willingness to ask for help and our desire for knowledge, we can become intelligent investors. Let's take a look at some of the best investing strategies and principles in the next few sections of this chapter.

A Few Nobel Prize Winners Can't Hurt

In this chapter I will introduce to you three different academic-based concepts which will help lay the groundwork for your investment strategy. Having a handle on three simple, common sense concepts will help you make solid investment decisions, both now and in the future. Once you understand these three concepts and how practically they apply to you, you will have a better understanding about investing.

Concept 1: Modern Portfolio Theory

Dr. Harry Markowitz created Modern Portfolio Theory (MPT) at the University of Chicago in the early 1950's. In 1990 when computer technology finally caught up with him and proved him right, Dr. Markowitz, along with William Sharpe and Merton Miller, won the Nobel Prize in Economics for the development of Modern Portfolio Theory. In order to explain this properly I'll need to define a few basic investing terms.

When we talk about investing, we naturally think of individual stocks, mutual funds, real estate or some other type of investments that we are either familiar with or that we have owned. For simplicity, in this explanation we are going to talk about stocks in general terms. Stocks are shares of an individual company, which represent partial ownership in that company. When you purchase a stock you are giving your money to a company who will then use your money to grow their business. In return for your investment you are entitled to a portion of the profit from said growth.

Every individual stock can be categorized into a larger group of similar stocks. We call these "asset classes" or categories. Examples of different asset classes are large U.S. companies, commonly represented by the S&P 500 maintained by Standard and Poor's, small U.S. companies, International large companies, International small companies and so on. When newspapers and television programs report on how "the market" is doing, typically they are referring to what large U.S. stocks are doing by citing the Dow Jones Industrial Average (DJIA), New York Stock Exchange (NYSE) or the Standard and Poor's (S&P 500).

Diversification—in Chick Terms

Diversification is being prepared for any situation. Imagine you are packing your suitcase for vacation but the weather where you are visiting is always unpredictable. You should pack sunglasses and a bathing suit for going to the beach, but you know it would be wise to bring an umbrella just in case you get caught in an unpredictable storm, or have to weather a hurricane. Think of Modern Portfolio Theory as packing your portfolio suitcase so that you are prepared for any kind of weather.

Let's Take a Closer Look at Modern Portfolio Theory

Historically, when you take a look at the various asset classes, you'll find that they all have various performance results at different times. When one particular category is performing poorly, another category might be performing well. The idea behind Modern Portfolio Theory is that by loading up your portfolio with distinct classes of investments that historically act differently; you can reduce the volatility or the amount of bouncing up and down in your portfolio when you diversify.

In the chart below there are two hypothetical investments that have similar volatility. If you owned just one of these two investments, you would experience the dramatic highs and lows from that investment. However, because these two investments don't move in the same direction at the same time, they have an opposite or negative correlation, and when combined in a 50/50 split portfolio, they level each other out and create a more consistent, steady return.

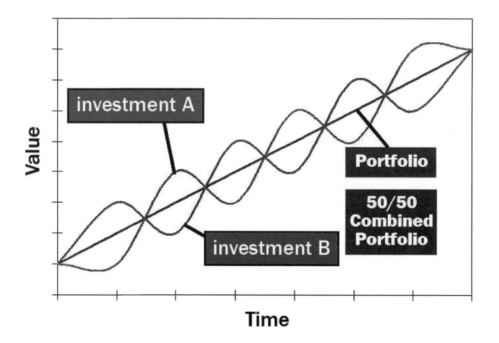

Getting the Most Bang for Your Buck (a.k.a. Portfolio Efficiency)

Another aspect of MPT is maximizing the bang for your buck. By combining these various asset classes, it is possible to increase your potential portfolio return, and stabilize or reduce your volatility at the same time. Dr. Markowitz established what is called the "Efficient Frontier," which shows the optimal level of possible return for any given level of risk tolerance.

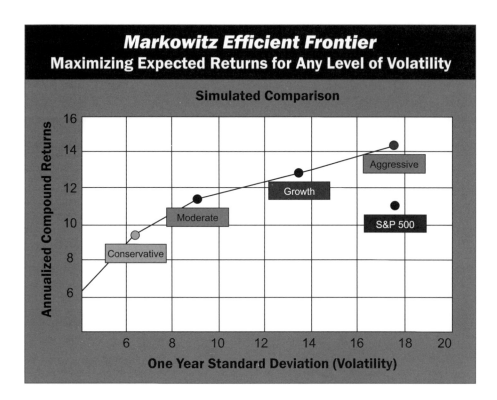

The graph above shows that by using diversification effectively you can maximize your potential return for your particular risk tolerance, which is measured by Standard Deviation. This is getting the most bang (return) for your buck (risk). Anytime you invest in the stock market you have to accept the ups and downs that go with it. However, with an efficient portfolio you can minimize the dramatic ups and downs as much as possible. I don't know about you, but I've had enough drama in my life without adding unnecessary risk to my financial future. Give me the slow and steady-eddy any day.

Concept 2: Efficient Market Theory

I am a child of the 80's so bear with me. As a child, whenever I saw a movie about investing or the stock market like *Wall Street* with Charlie Sheen and Michael Douglas, I was both intrigued and a little baffled.

One movie I remember vividly is *Quicksilver* with Kevin Bacon, not because it was a great movie, but because it made me think. I remember watching Bacon's character, a former stockbroker who had lost his parents' life savings and felt so bad about it that he became a bike messenger. Then Bacon returns to his "profession" as a stockbroker and makes numerous guesses regarding which stocks to buy based on his "feelings" about which ones were going to take off. When he first starts back as a stockbroker, he loses another batch of money, which belongs to one of his poor bike messenger friends who needs it because he is about to become a father. But somewhere along the way, he borrows a little more money, makes a good bet and makes tons of money in the stock market, all in one day. Everyone believes he has gotten his gift back and he becomes rich and the movie ends happily. It wasn't a great movie, but for some reason it got to me, and it irked me.

I never understood what made Bacon's character so outstanding. How did he know? Did he have some clairvoyant knowledge that one particular day, which everyone else missed? He was a bike messenger for crying out loud. I kept wondering if there were special schools where they taught him how to do this? Did God make him a remarkable guy? Were his insights into the stock market implanted randomly into his brain? Was it because he was smarter than everyone else? It didn't seem like it, since he had already lost a lot of his friends' and family's money doing the same thing, using the same exact method when he lost as he did when he had gotten lucky and won.

As a child, I dismissed the gut reaction I had. What did I know? I felt like there must be something that I was missing or couldn't comprehend. At the time, I accepted the fact that I was not mature enough to understand every aspect of why he got lucky and why he became rich so quickly. Once I was older, I went to work for my then fiancée's family in a financial planning practice, and I started learning more about the financial and investment industries.

I remember the first seminar I went to as an employee of the company, and my now brother-in-law Mark telling a particular group of clients that no one can predict the future of the stock market. That was the answer that I had been looking for in *Quicksilver*. It was the only thing that made sense. From that moment on, I knew that Kevin Bacon's character didn't have a special gift, and that he wasn't smarter than everyone else in the movie that were running around in little blue jackets and yelling really loud. It was simple; he was lucky. This helped me realize that sometimes people guess the stock market correctly, but at other times they guess it wrong. The difference is that when they are right, everyone wants them to continue to be right, so they elevate them into an investing genius. But when we put intelligence to work, we are cautious about relying on such flimsy predictions.

In an ironic side note, Kevin Bacon didn't learn any great investing secrets from his role in *Quicksilver*. In 2008, he and his wife, Kyra Sedgewick, were two of many victims of Bernie Madoff and his investment Ponzi scheme that cost investors over $50 billion.

There are three basic ways that traditional investment advice relies on predictions about the future to make decisions regarding investments. None of these methods stack up as statistically reliable or repeatable, and frankly, using them will only add more stress and anxiety to the investing process.

Stock Picking

Stock picking is predicting that a particular stock will perform differently in the future compared to how it is currently performing. Trying to find the one special company that is going to take off and outperform all of the rest is generally a losing battle. There are nearly 2,800 companies on the New York

Stock Exchange and about 3,200 in the NASDAQ. Do you think that someone knows which one, two or 10 of the approximate 6,000 stocks are going to be the biggest winners or losers in the next few months or years to come? Many times when you hear television analysts talking about an individual stock, they'll make a comment like "I'd place my bet on…" This statement is far more revealing than it seems. Stock picking in any form is nothing more than a bet. Stock picking is gambling on something unpredictable, which may or may not happen in the future. Do you want to gamble with your future? I know I don't, and I definitely don't need that added stress or pressure in my life.

Market Timing

The second predictive method used across the industry is "market timing," which happens any time a change is made to a portfolio based on what is currently hot, or on a prediction about the future. When it comes to money, it's easy to get caught up in what is happening today and lose sight of your long-term goals. Typically, market timing ends up looking like moving money in or out of a particular asset class based on current market conditions, which is usually motivated by one of two things—fear or greed. When a market is doing well, like the Technology stocks did in the late 90's, people want to load up and buy more of them because they don't want to be left out of the "boom of the decade," but that's primarily based on greed. When a market is doing poorly, like the United States Small Stocks faired in the mid-to-late 90's, people want to sell out and get as far away as possible, and this is based on fear. In both of these scenarios, the human survival instinct kicks in and dictates to us what to do. Unfortunately, it is the opposite of what we should do. In cases like this, we end up buying high or hot stuff and selling the poor performers – selling low. The only way to win in the market is to stay in it–all the time, even when it's a roller coaster.

For this particular Rich Chick analogy, imagine you work for a company and you have an unpredictable boss. Think of him or her as the stock market, where some days he or she is cranky, and you wish you had stayed at home. But on other days, he or she is over-the-top with generosity and crazy bonuses. If you worked for this company for 10 years and showed up every day to the equivalent of 2,520 workdays, your boss will have given you $22,252 in bonuses. However, if you missed only 10 days when he gave bonuses, you will only get $13,864 in bonuses. If you missed 20 bonus days, you'll only get $9,548...miss 30 days, $6,649... miss 40 days, $5,148...miss 60 days, you'll only receive $3,125.

If you miss 60 of the 2,520 days, that's only six days per year that you didn't show up to work. But, if they happen to be bonus days you would miss out on nearly 90% percent of the bonuses you could have received. My point is that if you want to reap the rewards the stock market has to offer, you have to show up and be in the game all of the time, because you never know when you are going to receive those bigger bonuses.

While this analogy gives you a sense of what missing the best days in the market can do, it's an imperfect example because in the stock market you also have days when you lose money. If you miss being in the market on the good days, you also miss chances to recoup losses from bad days.

January 1, 1996 – December 31, 2006 2,520 Trading Days		
	Return of S&P 500	**Growth of $10,000 Investment**
Fully Invested	8.33%	$22,252
Missed 10 best days	3.32%	$13,864
Missed 20 best days	-0.46%	$9,548
Missed 30 best days	-3.71%	$6,649
Missed 40 best days	-6.42%	$5,148
Missed 60 best days	-10.98%	$3,125

*Fact Set Research Systems
Based on initial investment of $10,000

> **Market timing does not work.**
> **It is just another way to gamble.**

Track-record Investing

Finally, there is another concept called "track-record investing," which is using past performance as a basis to determine if something is a good investment or not. In many circumstances in life, you can use the past as an indicator of what is likely to happen in the future. However, investing is not one of these occasions. In every investment prospectus, which is the fine print when it comes to investing, it clearly states in small but bold letters that "past performance is not indicative of future results." That is printed there for legal reasons, like the unpleasant side effects are listed on drugs; but in this case, it is almost always true.

The bottom line is that past performance doesn't tell us anything about the future when it comes to individual investments, so let's not waste our time on it.

If you hope to become a Rick Chick, this is so important for you to know and to accept. When it comes to investing, no one can predict what is going to happen in the future. Everything that affects market pricing is random and unpredictable. The stock market is not like a psychic hotline. No one knows what is going to happen tomorrow any more than the crazy folks on those late night commercials, who pretend to know what is going to happen in your future. The reason people believe that someone out there can pick the best stocks or investments or tell them what is going to happen in the market is because that's what they want to believe. They want reassurance that everything is not random and unpredictable. Much of our lives are unpredictable and random, just like the stock market. When we are looking for investment advice, we must be careful about whom we listen to, and we shouldn't trust everything we hear on television or radio or read about in a magazine, which may seem or sound believable.

When it comes to investing, we can't base our decisions on predictions. Think of it this way, if any of the people who make predictions or reports on television really knew what the next hot stock or investment was going to be, why on earth would they be on television telling you and the rest of the world about it? If they knew for sure, wouldn't they be on a private island somewhere, or on a yacht raking in the dough and living the luxurious life of the rich and famous? They wouldn't need to peddle their predictions to others. These supposed gurus make their money by convincing people to buy into what they're saying.

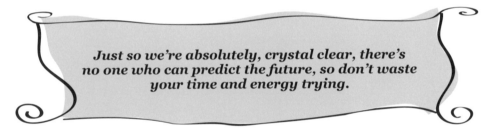

Just so we're absolutely, crystal clear, there's no one who can predict the future, so don't waste your time and energy trying.

No one can predict the future. Accepting this reality means you accept the idea that free markets work. It means that you don't believe in wasting time trying to outsmart a system that is already smarter than you are. It means that you buy into the economic principle of supply and demand, that the market will set stock prices appropriately, and that the price of a stock or investment today is the most accurate assessment of its value. Now we have simplified the "Efficient Market Theory." Fortunately, it doesn't take a psychic connection with super powers to become a highly successful investor, a Rich Chick or a millionaire. By using investment strategies that have been proven by math and history, you can put the "Efficient Market Theory" to work for you.

You have to decide for yourself what you believe. If you think there is someone out there smarter than the other 6.7 billion of us who can predict what's going to happen in the future, and that person is going to share that information with you, then this is not the book for you. If however, you are inclined to take a more practical and intelligent approach to your financial future, you are in the right place for gaining all of the knowledge you need to become a Rich Chick.

Asset Allocation

The good news is that you don't need any of the traditional investing methods to become a successful investor and a Rich Chick. The real substance in building a solid portfolio doesn't come from any of these tactics. Instead, a solid portfolio relies upon diversification and asset allocation. Like one of your favorite recipes, asset allocation is the mix of different asset classes within your portfolio.

Studies show that 91.5 percent of a portfolio's return is determined by asset allocation, and less than seven percent of a return can be attributed to stock picking, market timing and track-record investing. That means you should disregard much of what you see in the media regarding investments. The key to a solid strategy is based on sound economic principles.

What It All Means To You...

What this means to you is that in order to be a successful investor and a Rich Chick, you must diversify and pack your portfolio for every occasion. Markets work, which means that you don't need to depend upon shady predictions or recommendations about what the next hot stock or investment is going to be. And in order to reap the rewards of investing, you must be willing to take a certain amount of risk, which expectedly will reward you accordingly.

Rich Chick Review

How would you describe how Modern Portfolio Theory works?

_____

_____

_____

_____

What does diversification mean in Rich Chick terms?

_____

_____

_____

Why does the market work?

_____

_____

Rich Chick Tip:

Use the intelligence of the true experts of economics and investing when it comes to your financial future; don't rely on predictions or fortune-tellers.

Rich Chick Must-Have Accessory #7:

Intelligence ☑

Chapter Eight

The Down and Dirty on Investing...

Rich Chick Must-Have Accessory #8: Commitment

Now that we have a basic understanding of the underlying principles of economic theory relative to investing, it's time to dig further into the depths of the investment beast and reveal some of the mechanics of the process. You might be surprised how easy these things are to grasp once someone explains them in a way that's easy to understand. Your next Rich Chick Must-Have Accessory #8 is Commitment to the rules and the process. For someone like Donna and her husband, Commitment came naturally until the recent market downturns shook their resolve.

Real-Life Rich Chick: Donna

Donna and her husband, William, have been working with a financial advisor for years. They have put money aside in their retirement accounts and saved money for their children. When it comes to investing, they consider themselves experienced and usually feel good about how they are doing financially.

However, in a recent market downturn, even though they were well-diversified, Donna and William lost over twenty percent of what they had in their investment accounts last year. Although they realized that there was risk associated with their portfolio and investment goals, the reality of losing more than twenty percent hit them hard.

After suffering in silence for a couple of months and looking at their accounts online, Donna and William decided to visit their financial advisor. Their advisor Joe was very understanding and empathetic to their stress. However, when Donna and William suggested moving or selling their investments, Joe gently but firmly reminded them that this is what they had signed up for.

He explained that although this market downturn was stressful, their objective was the long-term growth of their assets and they still had many years until they would need their retirement money. Joe advised them that selling or moving their investments now was the only way to lock in the losses they had already experienced.

Logically, Donna and William knew he was right, and they agreed that they wanted the long-term benefits of stock market investing, but it was still uncomfortable for them to sit back and watch without doing anything while they were losing money. However, they stuck with it, and five years later they not only recouped all of their losses but also gained more return. In hindsight, they understood how disastrous it would have been if they had moved their money in panic. Donna and William are grateful that Joe kept them on the right track even when they wanted to do the wrong thing.

With commitment, as Donna and William learned, there are some very basic, standard rules when it comes to investing, and you've probably heard them before. Just like there are a couple of simple rules for losing weight by eating right and exercising, there are only three rules of investing that you must follow. However, like with losing weight, the rules get more complex as you dig deeper, so I'm going to do my best to keep things simple and as easy to understand as possible.

◎ ◎ ◎

The Three Simple Rules of Investing

1. *Own Equities*
2. *Diversify*
3. *Buy Low/Sell High*

Rule #1: Own Equities

Before we get into the specifics of the #1 Rule, which is to Own Equities, let's define the alternative, which is fixed income investments. Bonds, T-Bills and CDs are fixed income investments. They pay a fixed interest rate over a period of time. Traditionally, they are considered "safer" investments because they have a guaranteed return. However, historically, fixed income investments have a hard time keeping up with inflation, so the benefit goes away long-term.

Equities are stocks or stock-based mutual funds. The reason why it is so important to have at least a portion of your portfolio in equities is because they historically provide a much higher rate of return than fixed income investments, surpassing inflation. Stocks have inherently more risk, and therefore as a whole, provide a higher rate of return.

In the chart below, you will see the difference between the return you can historically expect from fixed income investments and equity investments. Not only is there a difference in the expected return, but there is also a difference in the amount of risk and volatility, which is measured by what's called Standard Deviation. Standard Deviation measures how much turbulence you can expect from an investment. The higher the standard deviation number, the more volatility and bouncing around you can expect from it.

1926–2008	T–Bills (Fixed Income)	S&P 500 (US Equity)
Annualized Return	3.70	9.62
Standard Deviation (volatility)	3.08	20.57

Source: DFA Returns Software 12/08

Holding equities in your portfolio is the only way you are going to pack enough punch, return-wise, to grow it into a million dollars. Fixed income investments should be used as a diversifier to offset volatility within your portfolio. The big question you will have to answer is to determine how much equity exposure you are willing to take in your portfolio. The answer to this question will vary depending on your risk tolerance and your age. The traditional moderate portfolio is considered a 60/40 mix—60 percent equity investments and 40 percent fixed. The more equity you put into your portfolio, the higher the expected volatility, and if done right, the more potential return.

Rule #2: Diversify

Diversification is a common financial term that is often misused and misunderstood. You may think that by simply owning a few different types of investments and not placing all of your money in one place that you are diversified, however, true diversification is much more than that. Real diversification is based upon maximizing your return potential while minimizing your volatility. It goes back to the asset classes that we discussed earlier.

Let's look at one example of how this works. If you own twenty different stocks, you aren't necessarily diversified. Because if those twenty different stocks are all part of the same larger asset category, they are likely to behave in a similar fashion, providing you no protection from volatility. Remember our sunglasses and umbrellas? Having many investments in the same asset category is similar to having twenty pairs of sunglasses—they just aren't going to help you when it rains. True diversification will enable you to be prepared for both sun and rain in unpredictable weather, because the stock market is unpredictable.

Once you have determined the amount of equity you want in your portfolio, then you must break that equity portion down into smaller segments to make sure that it is completely diversified. Different equity asset categories carry different amounts of volatility and anticipated return. When you start combining these investments, you can further increase your potential return and reduce your volatility, because they can offset each other.

Small Versus Large

Historically, small company stocks are riskier than large company stocks; but the silver lining lies in the fact that they typically provide a higher rate of return. When you include these in your portfolio, you can increase your return while stabilizing your volatility, because they don't do the same thing at the same time as the large company stocks do.

1926–2008	S&P 500	US Small Companies
Annualized Return	9.62	11.58
Standard Deviation (volatility)	20.57	39.16

Source: DFA Returns Software 12/08

Investing In U.S. Versus International Stocks

To achieve maximum diversification, it is vital to have a portion of your portfolio invested outside of the United States. International economies do not behave the same as the United States economy; therefore, they provide an additional layer of diversification inside your portfolio. Typical recommendations for how much you should own in international holdings in your portfolio range from 15 percent to 30 percent.

Value Versus Growth

When we break down investment types further, we end up with what are called value and growth stocks. Value stocks are companies who are struggling. These companies have a lower share price for their stocks compared to other companies of the same size or category. In an efficient market, these stocks are not undervalued, and there is no guarantee that they will catch up to similar companies, therefore, they historically offer a higher rate of return because they are inherently riskier.

July 1926–2008	S&P 500	US Large Value
Annualized Return	9.70	11.69
Standard Deviation	20.57	25.19

Source: DFA Returns Software 12/08

Keep in mind that there are some risks you won't be rewarded for, just as lottery tickets are not an investment. If you invest two dollars on a lottery ticket, your expected reward is a two-dollar loss, which is a negative return on your investment. Yes, someone has to win, but with chances so slim, it probably won't be you. Therefore, there is no reward for that kind of risk, so it is better to take your two dollars and put it into a real investment.

Rule #3: Buy Low/Sell High (Think Clearance)

Everyone loves a good deal. Imagine how it would feel to walk into a store and have an expensive purse jump into your arms at fifty percent off of the retail price. When you get a bargain like that, you feel like you've hit the jackpot of handbag heaven. As much as I would like this to happen to me, it never does. I am the worst bargain shopper on the planet. I think some people have the gift and others don't. I don't. I become completely overwhelmed by the stacks and racks of clearance items in any store. I'm much happier to shop off of the mannequin, instead of spending hours digging through stacks of wrinkled clothes that no one wanted in the first place. I know some women who are far more patient and cost conscious than I am. And I am always perplexed by how they find these amazing bargains. How do they do it?

When it comes to investing, investing in bargains and buying clearance items are essential to you. Shopping off of the investment mannequin means chasing whatever the hot stock or trend is, and that can mean portfolio suicide. When it comes to investing, the mannequin is whatever they are talking about on television or your media outlet of choice; and it usually has nothing to do with a good solid investment strategy. You'll always end up wearing last year's fashion if you shop or stop at what's hot in investing.

Rebalancing

There are actually bargains in investing too, and I think they are much easier to take advantage of if you have the right strategy. Everyone has heard the term "buy low/sell high." That is simple enough to understand, but harder to do when you're caught up in the stress and excitement of investing.

Once you have your portfolio designed, you only need to maintain it as you would a crock pot, and "let it cook." At times, it will become out of balance. Asset categories that have performed well will start to take up more of your portfolio, and they will eventually need to be sold off. Because they have been high performers, you will automatically be selling them at a higher rate when you rebalance.

The poor performers in your portfolio will have shrunk to a small percentage of the whole, so you will have to buy more of those. It may seem a little counterintuitive at first to buy assets that are performing poorly, but if you think of it as shopping off the clearance rack for your financial future, it will begin to make more sense.

A good investment strategy includes rebalancing. Rebalancing is like having a personal shopper for your portfolio, who is always finding you the best deal on name brand investments. Typically, a financial advisor or coach who is at work for you should be monitoring your portfolio on a regular basis to determine when and if any rebalancing is necessary.

Rich Chick Review

What are the three simple rules for investing?

1._____

2._____

3._____

When it comes to investing, why is it a good idea to make a long-term commitment?

_____

_____

_____

_____

What are the differences between small company and large company stocks?

_____

_____

_____

What does it mean to buy low and sell high? Why is this a good idea?

_____

_____

_____

Why does a good investment strategy involve rebalancing?

_____

_____

_____

Rich Chick Tip:

Sticking to the rules isn't always easy, but a Rich Chick sees the bigger picture and has the will to stick with the program.

Rich Chick Must-Have Accessory #8:

Commitment ☑

Chapter Nine

Cupcakes & Olympic Gold Medals...

Rich Chick Must-Have Accessory #9: Coachability

In the summer of 1984, as a wide-eyed eleven-year-old in utter amazement, I sat in front of the television watching Mary Lou Retton become the first U.S. gymnast to win the Olympic All-Around Gold medal in gymnastics. Like many other girls my age and the rest of America, I was fascinated by Mary Lou Retton and her accomplishments. In the years to come, I had clothing and other things plastered with her name and image all over my walls. She was and still is an inspiration to many people, because she is an ordinary girl from small-town West Virginia who did something amazing.

How did she do it? Well, she didn't do it by sitting around eating cupcakes and watching bad reruns, I can tell you that. Her coach, Bela Karolyi, who is one of the most well known gymnastics coaches to date, trained her for hours every day to help her become an Olympic Gold Medalist. All serious athletes who have the desire to compete have a grueling practice regimen, which allows them to achieve their goals. But do you think any of them would accomplish these things without the aid of a coach—hardly.

Do you think that Bela let Mary Lou sleep in, eat whatever she wanted, stay up late and show up to practice occasionally? If he had, Mary Lou wouldn't have achieved the same success. From the accounts I have read, Karolyi is one of the toughest coaches ever. And, there is no question that his coaching methods work. Mary Lou had a goal, Karolyi had a strategy and methodology to make it happen, and they agreed on the plan and worked the system together. He wasn't necessarily sweet and sympathetic; but without exception, his job was to instill discipline and a work ethic into Mary Lou to help her reach her goals.

If you're wondering what all of this has to do with investing, I wanted to give you a great example of how effective coaching works. In investing, just like in gymnastics, sticking with a plan is not always easy, even if you are committed to the goal. A person can be driven by purpose and determination, but still become sidetracked by life's distractions while trying to work their plan. Your investment goals are no different. Even with a strategy and a plan in place, it is easy to become a victim of what the media is throwing at you, or turn to other outside influences that can throw you off your game. My friend Karen learned the value of having a good investment coach, and you can make coachability work for you, too.

Real-Life Rich Chick: Karen

Karen is a person who considers herself a failure when it comes to properly managing her money. As early as grade school, she remembers that her allowance was always spent, even before she received it, and sometimes she borrowed against her future allowances. As she got older the rest of her finances fell into that same pattern—always living beyond her means and generally living with an overdrawn checking account on a daily basis. If you add up all the overdraft fees she's paid to the banks through the years, it would probably be enough to make her a millionaire.

So at the age of 36, when she was hired by a small printing firm, she began to listen to her coworkers and friends talk about retirement and their plans. After a friend mentioned it, she decided to start contributing to her company's 401(k). She thought it was absolutely awesome to watch her money grow and she was thankful to work for a company that was willing to match her contribution up to four percent. Karen often listened to stories about how other employees were retiring from that company after becoming millionaires just because they had invested in a 401(k). After several years of watching her money grow from a couple hundred dollars to approximately $18,000, she knew it was possible to retire a millionaire as well. She then made a huge financial blunder.

After seven years with the firm, there was a huge layoff, and unfortunately Karen was one of the many people that were let go. The company provided a wonderful severance package and they were very generous to those employees who were laid off. But instead of continuing to view her 401(k) plan as a long-term investment toward her future life in becoming a millionaire, she opted to withdraw the $18,000 instead of rolling it over into another retirement plan. By the time she paid the penalties and taxes on the money she took out, she was left with about half ($9,000) and that cash was gone so fast, she can't even remember how it was spent. On top of that, she ended up paying additional penalties to the IRS because she had withdrawn it early. Essentially, she paid the taxes on that money twice. And the worst part is that she knew all of the downfalls to withdrawing that money, but she did it anyway.

Now, she said making that decision was a horrible mistake. If she could just go back in time and rewrite history, she would leave the money in a 401(k) and sit back and watch it grow until she retires. Karen learned a valuable lesson from that huge financial blunder and she will choose not to make the same mistake again. She won't trade the momentary thrill of cash in her hand for the thrill of a secure, long-term, future investment.

Karen knows that the only thing predictable about life is that it is unpredictable. You never know what's around the corner. Unexpected life changes may tempt you to deviate from your investing plan. Changes in your job or financial situation are bound to come up, but you must be prepared to stick with your strategy, especially when the going gets tough.

In desperate times it may seem like dipping into your retirement funds is the only way to go. However, making up for lost ground and paying the penalties for touching your retirement funds too early are slippery slopes to tread on and you should be fully aware of the consequences that result in deviating from your plan.

If dieting and investing were easy, we would all be skinny and rich!

Have you ever noticed that two of the largest sections in a bookstore are the health/fitness/diet section and the money/finance section? Have you ever wondered why? Neither of these concepts are new, and typically most of the books have similar concepts, so why do we need so many books to make something happen? It's because there is a big difference between knowing what you need to do and doing it. Many people get lost somewhere in between having the knowledge of what to do and taking action.

What does it take to be fit and healthy? We all know the answer; there are two simple rules—eat right and exercise. So what's the problem? Why are so many people overweight and unhealthy? Because having the knowledge doesn't mean you are going to follow the rules. When you are trying to stay fit and healthy, it is easy to get sidetracked or led astray by the evils of everyday life. Who can resist chocolate chip cookies? With health and fitness, some people fall into bad habits, or have the lack of discipline, while other people are on the other end of the spectrum and hire a personal trainer who can help them stay on track.

When it comes to investing, think of yourself as an athlete who needs a personal trainer to keep her portfolio on track. It is just as easy to get sidetracked or manipulated when it comes to your investments as it is to eat a whole pint of mint chocolate chip ice cream when you're feeling blue. When the market is turbulent and the media is going to continue to make doom and gloom predictions, and it is easy to get sucked into that hype. Then you'll start questioning yourself and your strategy. A coach will help you stay focused on your game, your goals and the results you're trying to achieve with your investments. Like many other things in life, your investments are going to have good days and bad days. But your coach will help keep you focused when you need it, provide you with the education and information that you need to be comfortable and confident about your strategy, and help you find the right investment vehicles that will enable you to reach your goals. In regard to investing, the right coach will help you understand the important aspects of what you are doing and why. And just when you need it, your coach will give you a swift kick in the pants to help get your head on straight, by encouraging you to stick with your plan.

"Does this dress make my butt look big?"

In the history of the universe has a retail salesperson ever said, "Oh honey, please take that off, you look like a baby hippo in that thing?" I doubt it. The salesperson's job is to sell you something, and the more they sell to you the better. Do you need any accessories to go with that? Even if they are genuinely interested in helping you and making you feel good, they are motivated by something far more powerful than your needs or wants; they are getting paid, and money talks. They may believe some of the compliments they are dishing out to you, but they know that when you feel good about yourself you will spend more money.

Surprisingly, the world of investing isn't much different from your favorite retailer. The people who work at the large brokerage and investment companies aren't much different from the salesperson at the local boutique-clothing store at the mall. They both get paid when you buy something from them. But unlike the mall, the broker is selling you something that is far more elusive than a purse or a dress; they are selling you an idea, a prediction or a hope for your financial future, which is much more enticing and seductive than a pair of shoes.

When it comes to investing, sometimes you get what you pay for and sometimes you get taken. The commissions that the broker makes when he or she sells you an investment is only a fraction of what you might be paying to hold that investment. And sometimes you'll pay buried or hidden costs with your investments, and that's something to watch out for. As in the retail world, many times brokers who work in large investment companies work on commission. Commissions are simply a fee paid to the seller of an investment product when you purchase it. And, not all products pay the same amount of commission; some products are more lucrative for them to sell than others. Unfortunately, when it comes to investing, commissions are only the tip of the iceberg, in addition to other costs and expenses. Not everyone has your best interests at heart. You must be on the lookout for suspicious recommendations, and become fully aware of the process of purchasing investments, including who is getting paid and how.

There are other ways for someone other than you to make money off of your investments, which you might not notice if you don't know where to look. When it comes to your return, this could cost you a significant amount of money. As a whole, the financial industry doesn't want consumers to know about these costs, because they are the bread and butter that keeps their machine moving. We are not going to "ignore the man behind the curtain" today, ladies. We are going to figure out what makes this thing tick and see how we can go around the system and get the results we deserve for our investments.

After we take a look at commissions, the next thing we want to examine is the turnover. Turnover happens whenever unnecessary trading is occurring within an investment or portfolio. I'm going to use mutual funds as an example to explain how this works, but the concept is applicable across the board with all of your investments. According to the Securities Exchange Commission, "A mutual fund is a company that brings together money from many people and invests it in stocks, bonds or other assets. The combined holdings of stocks, bonds or other assets the fund owns are known as its *portfolio*. Each investor in the fund owns shares, which represent a part of these holdings."

Every mutual fund has turnover. Turnover is measured as a percentage and it measures the amount of changes the manager or the "genius" who decides which investments to hold in the fund makes to the investments within the fund. The higher the average turnover is within a fund, the higher the expense ratio (what it costs to run the fund).

Turnover increases expenses because of something called the bid/ask spread cost. The bid/ask spread is the difference between what you can buy a stock for (in dollars) and what you can sell it for. Stocks have a mark up; just like anything else you buy. The middle man, in this case the market maker, is the one skimming the "spread" in between. Every single trade made within a mutual fund is subject to the trading costs associated with the bid/ask spread, which sucks the return out of your portfolio every time a change is made inside the fund.

Bid/Ask Spread – In Chick Terms

I have a pair of shoes that I don't want anymore. They look fabulous, but they pinch my toes. You love my shoes and want to buy them, but in the investment world I can't sell my shoes directly to you. I have to go through a middleman called a "market maker;" which buys the shoes from me and sells them to you. The difference between the bid and the ask price is this: he will buy the shoes from me for $65, but he's going to turn around and sell the shoes to you for $80, keeping $15 for himself.

The average turnover in the typical United States Equity mutual fund is 114 percent per year. What that means is the manager has changed the investments in the funds over 100 percent.

Turnover – In Chick Terms

Imagine that you have put your trusted personal clothing consultant in charge of your amazingly chic walk-in closet, full of classic clothes, shoes and handbags that are timeless and always in fashion, while you go out of the country on a luxury spa vacation.

While you are gone, you call to check on your closet to make sure that your wardrobe is in good shape and all is well, and your trusted personal wardrobe advisor says that they've made some improvements that are going to make your wardrobe even better. You think this sounds great, so you go on about your business of relaxation and adventure.

When you arrive home a year later, you walk into your closet and find that your personal wardrobe consultant has sold everything you owned on consignment, for much less than you paid for it, and replaced it with all new things that you don't like or recognize. So, it has cost you not only the clothes that you had and liked, but also the difference between their value and what they were sold for, plus an extra 14 percent, because she bought more than you had originally purchased.

That is what happens to a mutual fund when the turnover is 114 percent. You buy a fund with a particular investment objective that is supposed to hold a specific type of investment. Over the course of the year, the manager of the fund buys and sells stocks or investments inside the fund, causing transaction fees that are subject to the bid/ask spread, and in effect are chipping away at any return the fund makes with each trade. By the end of a year, your fund holds totally different investments and may or may not look the same on the inside by the time it's all said and done.

To you and me, that doesn't make any sense. It violates the old "buy and hold" philosophy, making it impossible for you to fix-it-and-forget-it, because you are not in control of the ingredients in your own portfolio. If you are going to use mutual funds to build your portfolio, which can be a great option, it is imperative that you use funds with low turnover—funds that are in the 20 to 30 percent range. You also need to understand and know how to measure the internal expenses within your investments, because they will affect your bottom-line return.

Call me a control freak, but I'm not crazy about the idea of not knowing where the money that I'm investing is going. I'm also not excited about letting someone else, some active fund manager on Wall Street whom I've never met and doesn't have a clue about my life, make the decisions about the best ways to handle and invest my money.

Inside a mutual fund is not the only place in a portfolio where trading costs can eat away at your return and skyrocket expenses. Anytime there is activity in your portfolio; it is probably costing you more money. So, if you have a broker, a financial advisor, or if you're personally making frequent changes to or trades within your portfolio, then the return you are aiming for is being sabotaged by additional trading costs and expenses.

Fortunately, for us Rich Chicks there are ways to minimize and avoid many of these internal expenses, when we use cost effective mutual funds in our portfolio, and get the guidance we need to create a successful investment strategy that fits within our needs and our expectations.

The most effective way that I know of to get all of these things lined up is to find a good investor coach. It will be like having your own personal Bela Karolyi for your finances. Call it what you want, but you need someone who is going to do the dirty work for you, to sift through the loads of information that you don't need, and only deliver the essential information that you need to make sound investment choices.

A good investor coach is going to provide you with the education that is necessary for success. He or she will create a strategy that fits you, your goals and your needs, and will also instill the discipline you need to maintain your strategy for the long haul.

One of the key things that makes a true investor coach different from the brokers or advisors at large investment houses is that they work strictly off of fees. They don't earn commissions from products, which eliminates many conflicts of interest when it comes to the investment strategies they will recommend. You will gain more confidence in their recommendations if you aren't wondering if they are receiving a trip to Hawaii for recommending it to you. The elimination of commissions from the relationship means there is no hidden agenda for the coach. They are there to help you find a strategy that works and charge you a fee for doing so. Typically the fee is a percentage of your portfolio value; therefore, their only incentive is to make you more money, because if you are making more, they are earning more. It's a fair trade.

The second thing an investor coach has to offer that you won't get at a retail investment shop is educational opportunities. Many advisors have ongoing educational programs, which are designed to show you the information that is relevant to you and your strategy. You can feel good about being a student of a coach who is part of the process and understands what is going on.

Another quality of a true investor coach is that they have a firm investment philosophy they can articulate for you, so that you can decide whether it fits with your "True Purpose for Money" and your "Future View." They will also help you figure out what your investment philosophy is so that you can determine what works for you and eliminate all the clutter that doesn't line up with your philosophy.

Be certain that your coach recommends investment solutions and strategies which are backed up by the "smart guys," and their investment strategy and philosophy is backed up by economic theory and academic research. You don't want your coach to get hooked on what's hot or trendy in investing. You want them to use what works, historically, for the long run.

Finally, you want to make sure that your investor coach buys into your "True Purpose for Money" and "Future View" and is motivated to help you get there. A good coach will show a sincere interest in your goals and will help you develop a plan to get there.

What To Look For In An Investor Coach	
What to Look for:	**What to Avoid:**
Gets Paid by Fees	Earns Commission on Investment Products
Has a solid investment philosophy backed up by academic research	Uses a commercial slogan to explain his or her philosophy
Offers ongoing educational processes	Offers brochures and online reading
Understands and "gets" your True Purpose for Money	Offers you a "get rich quick" pill

Where To Look For A Good Investor Coach

There are many independent financial advisors in the world that have good hearts and truly want to help their clients. But figuring out which ones are "the good ones" is a bit of a challenge. It's similar to the concept of finding a good man. Even some good advisors aren't hip to the investment philosophy that we are covering here, so be prepared to ask them about and become familiar with their investment philosophy.

You may visit www.matsonmoney.com and obtain free materials that will help you make a solid choice about a good investor coach.

The materials and information that you will get from this site are rooted in the same investment philosophy, beliefs and strategies as the Rich Chick Method. You may also visit me at www.richchick.com.

Rich Chick Review

Why is it important to have a good coach?

_____

_____

_____

_____

What things should you look for in an investor coach?

_____

_____

_____

_____

What should you avoid?

_____

_____

_____

What can a good investor coach help you to do? What can they offer you?

_____

_____

_____

_____

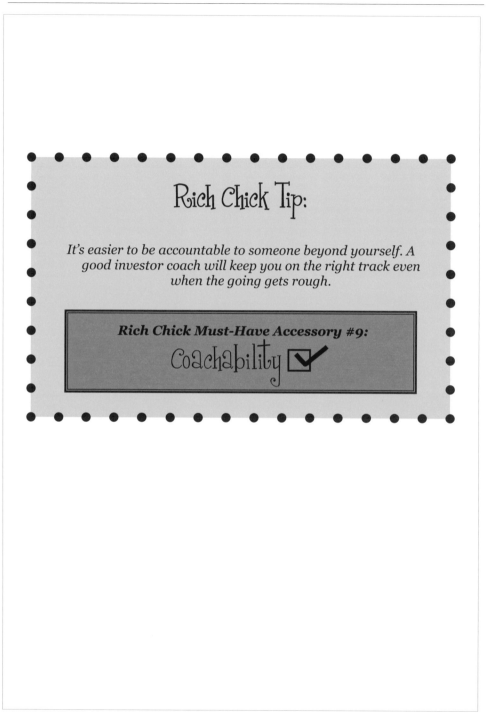

Rich Chick Tip:

It's easier to be accountable to someone beyond yourself. A good investor coach will keep you on the right track even when the going gets rough.

Rich Chick Must-Have Accessory #9:

Coachability ☑

Chapter Ten:

Happily Ever After...

The Rich Chick Method is applying all of the Nine Rich Chick Must-Have Accessories into place in your life, you'll soon be on your way to implementing a comprehensive, yet simple philosophy for becoming a Rich Chick. What do you get when you successfully apply these concepts? You become a real Rich Chick.

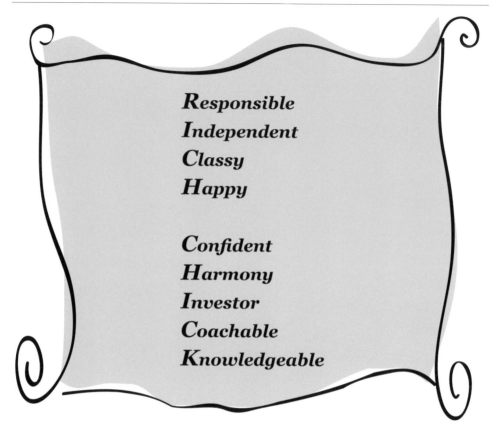

Responsible
Independent
Classy
Happy

Confident
Harmony
Investor
Coachable
Knowledgeable

Responsible

Congratulations! You are in charge of your own life and your future. You have taken hold of your destiny and you have all the power that goes along with it. No one else can either make or break your dreams...It's all you.

Independent

You are a strong woman who knows how to get what she wants out of life. You have everything it takes to make your own way in the world. You can take care of yourself and help others out along the way. You are your own heroine.

Classy

You are a classy, sassy lady who doesn't need to bend to the whims and trends of popular investment fashion. Your investment strategy and knowledge is timeless and true. You are above the noise of the media and the hype, and you have something that is better than trendy—you have peace of mind.

Happy

You create your own happiness with what you have. You work within your means and know that your savvy with investing is going to pay off.

Confidence

Working the Rich Chick Method gives you a confidence about money that permeates throughout every area of your life. Your sense of accomplishment gives you a boost that radiates from you.

Harmony

You know what your True Purpose for Money is and you are managing the rest of your life to fulfill that purpose. You have your priorities, goals, and values lined up to accomplish anything you set out to do.

Investor

A Rich Chick knows that investing in the stock market is the only way to grown your nest egg enough to keep up with and surpass inflation. Your strategy is grounded in a solid investment theory that will sustain over time.

Coachable

You know that doing the best thing for your financial future is not always an easy thing. A Rich Chick knows where to go for coaching and support, even when her instincts and outside circumstances drag her toward potentially making the wrong decision.

Knowledgeable

You have come farther in your education about investing and money than most people will ever go. Give yourself a pat on the back and feel good about your accomplishment. You have a base of knowledge that will put you on the right track to make smart decisions for years to come.

Your Happily Ever After is well within your grasp. I hope that by applying the Rich Chick Accessories that you are able to fulfill all of your dreams. The road to being a Rich Chick is an on-going journey that will keep you on your toes for years to come. It is a journey that is well worth the effort. And, the rewards will be more profound than anything merely about money.

Best of luck on your Rich Chick adventure, I'll be cheering for you all the way.

Rich Chick Glossary:

401(k) Plan

A qualified plan established by employers to which eligible employees may make salary deferral (salary reduction) contributions on a post-tax and/or pretax basis. Employers may make matching or non-elective contributions to the plan on behalf of eligible employees and may also add a profit-sharing feature to the plan. Earnings accrue on a tax-deferred basis.

Active Management

The use of a human element, such as a single manager, co-managers or a team of managers, to actively manage a fund's portfolio. Active managers rely on analytical research, forecasts and their own judgment and experience in making investment decisions on what securities to buy, hold and sell. The opposite of active management is called passive management, better known as "indexing."

Investors who believe in active management do not follow the efficient market hypothesis. They believe it is possible to profit from the stock market through any number of strategies that aim to identify mis-priced securities.

Investment companies and fund sponsors believe it's possible to outperform the market, and employ professional investment managers to manage one or more of the company's mutual funds. The objective with active management is to produce better returns than those of passively managed index funds. For example, a large cap stock fund manager would look to beat the performance of the Standard & Poor's 500 Index. Unfortunately, for a large majority of active managers, this has been difficult. This phenomenon is simply a reflection of how hard it is, no matter how smart the manager, to beat the market.

American Stock Exchange (AMEX)

The third largest stock exchange by trading volume in the United States, the AMEX is located in New York City and handles about 10 percent of all securities traded in the U.S.

Asset Class/Category

A type of investment, such as stocks, bonds, real estate or cash.

Asset Allocation

An investment strategy that aims to balance risk and reward by apportioning a portfolio's assets according to an individual's goals, risk tolerance and investment horizon. The three main asset classes (equities, fixed-income, and cash and equivalents) have different levels of risk and return, so each will behave differently over time.

Bid/Ask Spread

The amount by which the ask price exceeds the bid. This is essentially the difference in price between the highest price that a buyer is willing to pay for an asset and the lowest price for which a seller is willing to sell it. For example, if the bid price is $20 and the ask price is $21 then the "bid-ask spread" is $1.

Bonds

A debt investment in which an investor loans money to an entity (corporate or governmental) that borrows the funds for a defined period of time at a fixed interest rate. Bonds are used by companies, municipalities, states and the U.S. and foreign governments to finance a variety of projects and activities.

Bonds are commonly referred to as fixed-income securities and are one of the three main asset classes, along with stocks and cash equivalents.

Certificate of Deposit (CD)

A savings certificate entitling the bearer to receive interest. A CD bears a maturity date, a specified fixed interest rate and can be issued in any denomination. CDs are generally issued by commercial banks and are insured by the FDIC. The term of a CD generally ranges from one month to five years.

Commissions

A service charge assessed by a broker or investment advisor in return for providing investment advice and/or handling the purchase or sale of a security. Most major, full-service brokerages derive most of their profits from charging commissions on client transactions. Commissions vary widely from brokerage to brokerage.

Compounding

The ability of an asset to generate earnings, which are then reinvested in order to generate their own earnings. In other words, compounding refers to generating earnings from previous earnings.

Correlation

In the world of finance, a statistical measure of how two securities move in relation to each other. Correlations are used in advanced portfolio management.

Diversification

A risk management technique that mixes a wide variety of investments within a portfolio. The rationale behind this technique contends that a portfolio of different kinds of investments will, on average, yield higher returns and pose a lower risk than any individual investment found within the portfolio.

Diversification strives to smooth out unsystematic risk events in a portfolio so that the positive performance of some investments will neutralize the negative performance of others. Therefore, the benefits of diversification will hold only if the securities in the portfolio are not perfectly correlated.

Efficient Frontier

A line created from the risk-reward graph, comprised of optimal portfolios.

Equities

1. A stock or any other security representing an ownership interest.
2. In terms of investment strategies, equity (stocks) is one of the principal asset classes. The other two are fixed-income (bonds) and cash/cash-equivalents. These are used in asset allocation planning to structure a desired risk and return profile for an investor's portfolio.

Fixed Income

A type of investing or budgeting style for which real return rates or periodic income is received at regular intervals at reasonably predictable levels. Fixed-income budgeters and investors are often one and the same—

typically retired individuals who rely on their investments to provide a regular, stable income stream. This demographic tends to invest heavily in fixed-income investments because of the reliable returns they offer.

Growth Stocks

Shares in a company whose earnings are expected to grow at an above-average rate relative to the market. Also known as a "glamour stock."

Inflation

The rate at which the general level of prices for goods and services is rising, and subsequently, purchasing power is falling.

Individual Retirement Account (IRA)

An investing tool used by individuals to earn and earmark funds for retirement savings. There are several types of IRAs: Traditional IRAs, Roth IRAs, SIMPLE IRAs and SEP IRAs.

Traditional and Roth IRAs are established by individual taxpayers, who are allowed to contribute 100 percent of compensation (self-employment income for sole proprietors and partners) up to a set maximum dollar amount. Contributions to the Traditional IRA may be tax deductible depending on the taxpayer's income, tax filing status and coverage by an employer-sponsored retirement plan. Roth IRA contributions are not tax-deductible.

SEPs and SIMPLEs are retirement plans established by employers. Individual participant contributions are made to SEP IRAs and SIMPLE IRAs.

Market Timing

1. The act of attempting to predict the future direction of the market, typically through the use of technical indicators or economic data.

2. The practice of switching among mutual fund asset classes in an attempt to profit from the changes in their market outlook.

Mutual Fund

A mutual fund is a company that brings together money from many people and invests it in stocks, bonds or other assets. The combined holdings of stocks, bonds or other assets the fund owns are known as its *portfolio*. Each investor in the fund owns shares, which represent a part of these holdings.

NASDAQ

A computerized system that facilitates trading and provides price quotations on more than 5,000 of the more actively traded over the counter stocks. Created in 1971, the NASDAQ was the world's first electronic stock market.

Stocks on the NASDAQ are traditionally listed under four- or five-letter ticker symbols. If the company is a transfer from the New York Stock Exchange, the symbol may be comprised of three letters.

New York Stock Exchange (NYSE)

A stock exchange based in New York City, which is considered the largest equities-based exchange in the world based on total market capitalization of its listed securities. Formerly run as a private organization, the NYSE became a public entity in 2005 following the acquisition of electronic trading exchange Archipelago. The parent company of the New York Stock Exchange is now called NYSE Euronext, following a merger with the European exchange in 2007.

Also known as the "Big Board," the NYSE relied for many years on floor trading only, using the open outcry system. Today, more than half of all NYSE trades are conducted electronically, although floor traders are still used to set pricing and deal in high volume institutional trading.

Passive Management

A style of management associated with mutual and exchange-traded funds (ETFs) where a fund's portfolio mirrors a market index. Passive management is the opposite of active management in which a fund manager(s) attempts to beat the market with various investing strategies and buying/selling decisions of a portfolio's securities.
Also known as "passive strategy," "passive investing" or "index investing."

Portfolio

A grouping of financial assets such as stocks, bonds and cash equivalents, as well as their mutual, exchange-traded and closed-fund counterparts. Portfolios are held directly by investors and/or managed by financial professionals.

Return

The gain or loss of a security in a particular period. The return consists of the income and the capital gains relative on an investment. It is usually quoted as a percentage.

Risk

The chance that an investment's actual return will be different than expected. This includes the possibility of losing some or all of the original investment. Risk is usually measured by calculating the standard deviation of the historical returns or average returns of a specific investment.

Risk Tolerance

The degree of uncertainty that an investor can handle in regard to a negative change in the value of his or her portfolio.

Roth IRA

An individual retirement plan that bears many similarities to the traditional IRA, but contributions are not tax deductible and qualified distributions are tax-free. Similar to other retirement plan accounts, non-qualified distributions from a Roth IRA may be subject to a penalty upon withdrawal.

Securities Exchange Commission (SEC)

A government commission created by Congress to regulate the securities markets and protect investors. In addition to regulation and protection, it also monitors the corporate takeovers in the U.S. The SEC is composed of five commissioners appointed by the U.S. President and approved by the Senate. The statutes administered by the SEC are designed to promote full public disclosure and to protect the investing public against fraudulent and manipulative practices in the securities markets. Generally, most issues of securities offered in interstate commerce, through the mail or on the Internet must be registered with the SEC.

Standard Deviation

1. A measure of the dispersion of a set of data from its mean. The more spread apart the data, the higher the deviation. Standard deviation is calculated as the square root of variance.

2. In finance, standard deviation is applied to the annual rate of return of an investment to measure the investment's volatility. Standard deviation is also known as historical volatility and is used by investors as a gauge for the amount of expected volatility.

Stock

There are two main types of stock: common and preferred. Common stock usually entitles the owner to vote at shareholders' meetings and to receive dividends. Preferred stock generally does not have voting rights, but has a higher claim on assets and earnings than the common shares. For example, owners of preferred stock receive dividends before common shareholders and have priority in the event that a company goes bankrupt and is liquidated.

Also known as "shares" or "equity."

Stock Market (The "Market")

The market in which shares are issued and traded either through exchanges or over-the-counter markets. Also known as the equity market, it is one of the most vital areas of a market economy as it provides companies with access to capital and investors with a slice of ownership in the company and the potential of gains based on the company's future performance.

Stock Picking/Selection

A situation in which an analyst or investor uses a systematic form of analysis to conclude that a particular stock will make a good investment and, therefore, should be added to his or her portfolio. The position can be either long or short and will depend on the analyst's or investor's outlook for the particular stock's price.

Treasury Bills (T-Bills)

A short-term debt obligation backed by the U.S. government with a maturity of one year or less. T-Bills are sold in denominations of $1,000 up to a maximum purchase of $5 million and commonly have maturities of one month (four weeks), three months (13 weeks) or six months (26 weeks).

T-Bills are issued through a competitive bidding process at a discount from par, which means that rather than paying fixed interest payments like conventional bonds, the appreciation of the bond provides the return to the holder.

Track-record Investing

Using an investment's performance in the past as an indicator of whether it will perform well in the future.

Turnover

1. In accounting, the number of times an asset is replaced during a financial period.
2. The number of shares traded for a period as a percentage of the total shares in a portfolio or of an exchange.

Value Stocks

The strategy of selecting stocks that trade for less than their intrinsic values. Value investors actively seek stocks of companies that they believe the market has undervalued. They believe the market overreacts to good and bad news, resulting in stock price movements that do not correspond with the company's long-term fundamentals. The result is an opportunity for value investors to profit by buying when the price is deflated.

Typically, value investors select stocks with lower-than-average price-to-book or price-to-earnings ratios and/or high dividend yields.

Volatility

A statistical measure of the dispersion of returns for a given security or market index. Volatility can either be measured by using the standard deviation or variance between returns from that same security or market index. Commonly, the higher the volatility, the riskier the security.

Glossary definitions courtesy of <u>www.investopedia.com</u>.

Notes

*Chapter 4: determination. (2009). In *Merriam-Webster Online Dictionary*.

Retrieved January 28, 2009, from http://www.merriam-webster.com/dictionary/determination

Rich Chick Research

Bach, David. Smart Women Finish Rich. New York: Broadway Books, 1999.

Burton, G. Malkiel. A Random Walk Down Wall Street. New York: W.W. Norton & Company, 2003.

Chatzky, Jean. Make Money Not Excuses. New York: Three Rivers Press, 2006.

Ellis, D. Charles. Winning the Loser's Game. New York: McGraw Hill, 2002.

Frankel, P. Lois. Nice Girls Don't Get Rich. New York: Hachette Book Group USA, 2005.

Schultheis, Bill. The Coffeehouse Investor. Kirkland, WA: Palouse Press,1998.